REES HOWELLS
Intercessor

REES HOWELLS
Intercessor

By

Norman Grubb

" He staggered not at the promise of God through unbelief; but was strong in faith, giving glory to God."

ROM. 4:20

CHRISTIAN LITERATURE CRUSADE
Fort Washington, Pennsylvania 19034

CHRISTIAN LITERATURE CRUSADE

U.S.A.
P.O. Box 1449, Fort Washington, PA 19034

GREAT BRITAIN
51 The Dean, Alresford, Hants., SO24 9BJ

AUSTRALIA
P.O. Box 91, Pennant Hills, N.S.W. 2120

NEW ZEALAND
10 MacArthur Street, Feilding

ISBN 0-87508-188-6

Copyright © 1952
Lutterworth Press

First published 1952
New cover added 1993
This Printing 1996

This trade-size American edition
by special arrangement with
the British publishers.

Cover photo credit: SuperStock

PRINTED IN THE UNITED STATES OF AMERICA

Contents

Chapter		Page
	FOREWORD	7
1.	EARLY YEARS	11
2.	TWO SHOCKS	17
3.	MEETING THE RISEN LORD	21
4.	THE WELSH REVIVAL	29
5.	THE HOLY SPIRIT TAKES POSSESSION	33
6.	LOVING AN OUTCAST	41
7.	A VILLAGE UNTOUCHED BY THE REVIVAL	49
8.	THE TRAMPS	55
9.	BINDING THE STRONG MAN	63
10.	A BRANCH IN THE VINE	69
11.	THE TUBERCULAR WOMAN	73
12.	WHAT IS AN INTERCESSOR?	81
13.	CHALLENGING DEATH	87
14.	A FATHER TO ORPHANS	91
15.	LORD RADSTOCK	97
16.	CALLED TO A HIDDEN LIFE	101
17.	THE HATLESS BRIGADE	107
18.	THE VOW OF A NAZARITE	113
19.	UNCLE DICK'S HEALING	121
20.	CALLED OUT FROM WAGE-EARNING	127
21.	MADEIRA	131
22.	MARRIAGE AND MISSIONARY CALL	141
23.	STANDING IN THE QUEUE	149
24.	REVIVALS IN AFRICA	155
25.	BUYING THE FIRST ESTATE IN WALES	173
26.	THE BIBLE COLLEGE OF WALES	185
27.	BUYING THE SECOND ESTATE	189
28.	THIRD ESTATE AND CHILDREN'S HOME	195
29.	THE BOOK OF COMMON PRAYER AND KING EDWARD VIII	201
30.	THE EVERY CREATURE COMMISSION	205

31.	ETHIOPIA	211
32.	VISITATION OF THE SPIRIT	217
33.	FOURTH ESTATE AND THE JEWS	223
34.	INTERCESSION FOR DUNKIRK	231
35.	THE BATTLE OF BRITAIN	241
36.	RUSSIA, NORTH AFRICA, ITALY, "D" DAY	247
37.	HOME CALL	259

Foreword

I count it as one of the great privileges of my life to have had a hand in preparing this biography of Rees Howells. I first met Mr. Howells in 1928. I was then a missionary on furlough, and as I spent a few days with him at the Bible College of Wales, which was then in its young days, light simply poured into my soul as he took time to tell me some of the Lord's inner dealings with him. It was one of the great experiences of my life. I learned secrets of the Spirit—as the One come down to do His mighty work through human agents—which revolutionized my future ministry.

In the years that followed I had many periods of intimate fellowship with Mr. Howells, although I always wondered why I was allowed such a privilege, and it came to my mind on many occasions how much I would like to get that testimony, that light the Lord had revealed to His servant, those marvelous dealings of the Spirit with him, into print for the world. It now seems as if it was an unrecognized preparation for what was coming. I never dreamed that the Lord would so suddenly take His servant; but as soon as I heard, back came those thoughts of past years.

It was because of this that Samuel Howells, Mr. Rees Howells' only son, and Mrs. Rees Howells, offered me the great honor of writing his life. But I now want to make it clear that I have only been, as it were, the senior member of a writing team. First, Miss Mary Henderson, Mr. Howells'

honorary secretary, for the past ten years had faithfully recorded his morning and evening talks in the college—eighty manu-
script books of them and packed with references to his own experiences—and then in preparation for the biography had
spent weeks in indexing them, so that I could get straight to the
important passages. We have been daily co-workers in preparing the book, and she has been able to keep me on the straight
and narrow path of accuracy on many points, and add vital
tid-bits of information.

Then Dr. Kingsley Priddy, the headmaster of the Bible College School, has dedicated hours of his time to going over every
chapter and offering many valuable suggestions. With his keenly sensitive appreciation of the spiritual content of Mr.
Howells' life, he has been able again and again to put the needed touch to bring out the inner essence of an incident.

Combined with this has been the work of Miss Marie Scott,
B.A. As teacher of English literature in the School and College, as well as being one of those whose life was revolutionized
through her contacts with Mr. Howells, she has smoothed out
many an uncouth passage, and often added touches of inspiration.

Miss Doris Ruscoe, B.A., the headmistress, has been
another member of the team and helped particularly in ham-
mering out the best methods of producing the biography; and
finally, all has been checked by Mr. Samuel Howells, M.A.,
the present Director of the Bible College, and by Mrs. Rees
Howells, who was with her husband from the earliest days of
his ministry and was herself eyewitness of a great deal recorded
in the book.

I have found it a most healthy and exhilarating experience
to produce a book as a team instead of as an individual, and
we have been wonderfully conscious every day of the Lord's
good hand on us.

For some of the facts of Rees Howells' early days, we have
been indebted to his eldest brother, Mr. John Howells, who
was always greatly respected by the family, and to another
brother, Mr. Dick Howells, a retired mine-manager, and to his

sister, Nurse Catherine Howells, who was deeply devoted to him, and to Mr. Tom Howells, the only remaining member of the family still living in the old home.

Beyond measure large-hearted, irrepressible in the joy of the Lord which poured out of him ("The Spirit is full of jokes," he once daringly said), this man of God, who bore on his heart the world's deep suffering and sin till it broke him, could have told his own tale with so much more vividness than we could ever put into it; but may God reveal, even through these pages, Himself through the veil of human flesh, through a man "changed into the same image from glory to glory, even by the Spirit of the Lord."

Mr. Morgan James, a retired official of the Great Western Railway, and a friend of Mr. Howells, well said, "He was the biggest-hearted Christian I ever met." The men of God of his generation recognized the peculiar anointing of God upon him: Lord Radstock; Mr. Albert Head, the chairman of the Keswick Convention; Mr. D. E. Hoste, the director of the China Inland Mission; Mr. Stephen Jeffreys, so mightily used in evangelism and healing, who in his last years leaned much on Mr. Howells' faith; Mr. Dan Williams, founder of the Apostolic Church; Mr. Paget Wilkes of the Japan Evangelistic Band; the Rev. Andrew Murray, who wrote of him in a booklet and asked him to come for a visit; Miss Bentham of Dr. Barnardo's; Mrs. Charles Cowman, author of *Streams in the Desert*.

Mr. Henry Griffiths, a Group Accountant of the National Coal Board, said this of his first acquaintance with him in 1921: "I read about the mighty movement of the Spirit through him in Africa. He was coming to Llanelly, so I walked three miles to hear him. He was to me the most wonderful missionary I had read of. His way of speaking was different, the Spirit had so dealt with him. I remember one young Christian asking him how he knew God's voice, and he said, 'Can't you tell your mother's voice from any other?' 'Yes, of course,' the young man answered. 'Well, I know His voice just like that.' I shall never forget the meetings in the Llandrindod Convention after he came back from Africa. Frankly, he was by himself. He was only about forty years old and in the strength of his manhood. He lifted the meeting to such a plane that everyone was spellbound. No one could move, no one could follow him. He was requested to test the meeting and asked who would like to give themselves to God as he had done, and everyone stood up, ministers and all. At a ministers' meeting the next day, to which I was allowed to come, Mr. Paget Wilkes was speaking. He was quick enough to recognize the Spirit in Mr. Howells, and said, 'There is someone here among us, and I feel like going round the country with him, carrying his bag and cleaning his boots.' "

May God meet with many in reading this book, as He has met with the author in writing it.

Norman P. Grubb

1

Early Years

Rees Howells was born on October 10, 1879, the sixth of a family of eleven. The little white-washed cottage still stands on the Llandilo Road, in the mining village of Brynamman, South Wales, where Thomas and Margaret Howells brought up three girls and eight boys. It is a wonder that the little home could contain them!

It was a hard struggle in the early years. Rees' father had employment in the iron works, and afterwards in a coal mine. His wages, the sole source of income for the family, was the handsome sum of 2s. 3d. or 2s. 6d. a day, and sometimes, when a strike was on, there would be nothing at all, and no Unemployment Benefit. In later years he opened a little shop in the village for the sale and repair of shoes, and things became easier as the older children left school and went to work.

But they were a happy family, for godliness and love were pre-eminent in the home. His mother's love was one of the deepest impressions on Rees' young life, especially as he watched her ceaselessly nursing one of the three little members of their circle who were later taken from them. As for the proud father, a visitor one day puzzled young Rees by looking round on all the children and exclaiming to his father, "How rich you are!" "How could he say you are rich?" Rees asked him later. "Well, how much would I sell you for?" answered his father. "For £1,000? Or would I sell John, David or Dick for £1,000 each? That's how rich I am!"

Most of the children started work in the local tin mill, at the bottom of the valley below the village. The only education they had was in the one village school. They were not supposed to be employed before they were thirteen years old, but when Rees was only twelve and was taking food down to his brothers in the mill, the manager asked him one day if he would like to do a little work. His name would not be on the pay roll, but he would give him a wage and put it down in the name of his brother Moses. So Rees' schooling ended at twelve, and the next ten years were spent in the tin mill, where he was considered a good worker. His job claimed him for twelve hours a day, rising at 6 a.m. and not returning home till nearly 6 p.m.

Both Rees and his brothers felt their need for further education and attended night classes weekly in the village school. In those days there was no such thing as a library in the village; the only reading center was a little newspaper shop, where for a penny a month they could go and read the newspaper or borrow a book. By these means two of his brothers passed several examinations, John, the eldest, joining the Railway Company, and Dick becoming a colliery manager.

Rees himself did not take up any specific line of study, but he did show signs of organizing capacity. When his mother would give the boys odd jobs to do, the others would each do their own, but Rees would usually manage to get about half a dozen of his friends to help him—and then ask his mother to give them all dinner! She must have wondered if it was worth asking Rees to do a job!

The generosity which was such a marked characteristic of his later life was also to be seen in his boyhood days. He would give all he had away. One of his brothers tells how a customer came into the shop to buy some shoes while his father was absent. The customer tried to persuade this brother to reduce the price from 3s. 9d. to 2s. 6d., but he refused. A few days later she came in and told the story to his father, giving a description of "the salesman," which could fit either Rees or the brother. It didn't take the father a second to choose, for he knew Rees couldn't have refused her!

Rees developed a fine physique, and was interested in physical training. He brought home dumbbells, boxing gloves, and so on, and took his brothers on in friendly fights. A healthy appetite accompanied a healthy body. Dick and Rees arrived back late some nights from their various occupations. If Dick came in first, so the story goes, his mother who had gone upstairs would call down, "Is that you, Dick? Help yourself to a piece of tart." But if Rees preceded Dick, his mother would call down, "Is that you, Rees? There's a tart on the table. Leave a piece for Dick!"

But outstanding from Rees' earliest days was his consciousness of God. It seemed as if an invisible Presence overshadowed him from birth, the One who, as with Paul, separated him from his mother's womb and called him by His grace. In this respect Rees' grandparents were the most powerful influence on his early years. Their home was another little white-washed cottage, called Pentwyn, up on the Black Mountain, and to cross their threshold, Rees said in later years, was to pass from earth to heaven. They had been converted in the 1859 Revival, and Rees always believed that their blessing came down to him. Something drew him in that little home: "God was its atmosphere," he would say. He loved the walk from his own home down in the Amman Valley, up through the fields, leaving the houses behind one by one, until an iron gate clanged behind him, and he was out in the silent spaces of the mountain slopes, which in future years were so often to be his trysting place with God. Here the only sounds that disturbed the stillness were the song of the lark, the occasional bleating of sheep, and the music of tumbling mountain stream.

Over the crest young Rees would go, down the other side, with the eight miles of green Welsh valley spread out before him, till he reached his beloved Pentwyn, perched on the steep slopes where the moorland gave place again to hedges and fields. As he crossed the threshold, he would usually hear the sound of his grandmother's voice reading the Bible to his invalid Uncle Dick. It reminds us of another young lad who probably spent many an hour on another Black Mountain,

Kara-Dagh, with Lystra at its foothills, where young Timothy was brought up under the godly influence of his "grandmother Lois and his mother Eunice."

Indeed, the young men of Bible times, like Joseph and David, who feared and served God from their boyhood days, had a great influence on Rees. His wise father had brought the children up on the Bible stories; Rees' earliest memories were of those evening readings and their effect on him. The story of the Savior, His birth and life and death, stood out above all others, and kept him from ever taking His name in vain or daring to sin against Him.

Even the normal pleasures of the world had no attraction for him. He would walk miles to hear someone preach and bring him "under the influence of God," but he "wouldn't cross the road to hear a concert." Only once did he even attend a football match. As the crowd were "shouting and bawling" around him, he felt it was not the place for him, and vowed that, when he got his feet out of it, he would never go to such a place again. He never did.

The Apostle Paul makes that striking statement about serving God, as did his forefathers, with pure conscience, and Rees seemed another example of it. "I didn't run into sin," he said years later. "There was always a restraint on me. It seems that some people are much more sensitive than others, even before conversion. I marred my conscience once, when my father sent me to deliver some shoes to a customer, and I asked him for 1s. 10d. when the correct price was 1s. 9d. I spent the penny on apples. Although I confessed my sin to my father, I never got it out of my mind—especially when I saw apples! I had marred my conscience. Of course, because it had that effect on me, it kept me from anything bigger." But it also had another effect, from which he had to be disillusioned later, for he added, "I thought in those days that probably I had been born with a good nature!"

He became a member of the chapel at thirteen, resolving, according to the light he then had, that he must now "live up to the teaching of the Savior." He got this idea from reading

Sheldon's book *In His Steps*, only to find out later, of course, that he couldn't do it.

Contact with the other young fellows in the tin mill did not alter his tastes. Swansea was only about twenty miles away, but "city life, a superficial life, never appealed to me," he said. "It was no test to me not to go to a theatre; I didn't like such places. I was at home in the chapels and prayer meetings. Nature—the hills and valleys and running streams—appealed to me. Sunday mornings were wonderful times to me: such a hush and peace over everything. I felt I could face God every night, because I lived such a clean, pure life, and there were hundreds in Wales who lived like that."

Quiet, good living, hard working; there was not much to attract attention to this young Welsh lad or to inspire prophecies for the future, except perhaps an unusual piety, which might be strange to English eyes though maybe not to Welsh. But is it not God who turns the ordinary into the extraordinary when He is given a chance?

2

Two Shocks

Not until Rees was twenty-two did anything happen to alter the quiet course of his life at home. By then he was a fine-looking, broad-shouldered young man of nearly six feet, with sensitive hands, the striking square-cut forehead which one sometimes sees among the Welsh; and above all, remarkable eyes, crystal clear and penetrating: the eyes of a seer. Beneath the quiet surface, however, one strong tide was running — ambition. He wanted to see the world, he wanted to make money, and America became the loadstone. Several young men from the village had gone to the U.S.A. and were sending back glowing reports of the money they were making, earning in one day what it would take a week to get in South Wales.

When Rees heard this, nothing could hold him back, not even the pull of home. He "weighed the losses and gains, and America won every time." His brothers were studying for careers, but he decided "to make money and retire early in life"! He had a cousin, Evan Lewis, who had emigrated and taken work at New Castle, in the steel area around Pittsburgh, and Rees took ship and joined him, getting employment in a tin mill.

Before he left Brynamman, however, a word from God came to him, which he called the greatest blessing he received before his conversion. One Sunday night, a month before he sailed, he came late to church, and as it was crowded out, he stood in the vestibule. The minister was reading Hebrews 12:1.

"Wherefore, seeing we also are compassed about with so great a cloud of witnesses . . . ." "These witnesses," he said, "are the men of faith mentioned in the previous chapter and we ought to realize they are around us; we know they are real, because Moses and Elijah spoke to the Savior on the Mount of Transfiguration, and the disciples saw them." The minister then said straight out, just as if he knew Rees was listening, "Young man, you may be leaving home, you may be going to a place where your parents will not see you; but remember, the cloud of witnesses and God will see you."

The words struck home to Rees. They were new to him and the effect was "an impression from the other world" coming over him. "I saw the Mount of Hebrews 12:22," he said, "the city of the living God, the general assembly and church of the first-born." He saw them, not as spies, but there to encourage and strengthen him. It was God's overshadowing Hand again, putting an external restraint on His chosen vessel, until He revealed His Son to him; for till that day came, this cloud of witnesses remained "the greatest reality" of his life.

When he left his homeland Rees continued to live the same religious life in America, where he became a member of a church and never missed a prayer meeting. Only once did he nearly yield to the temptation of worldly amusements, when a friend invited him to go to a big boxing match. Doubtless his former interest in boxing was the attraction. But the Restraining Hand was upon him. The day before the match, the thought came to him, "If your father or uncle were here, would you go? And what about the cloud of witnesses?" He told his friend he wouldn't accompany him that night for a fortune!

Living an upright life like that, how could God bring him to the realization that he was born in sin and needed to be saved? Even the minister of his church thought he was "the best young man in the congregation"—an indication that the minister himself must have needed what Rees needed! His case was not unlike Paul's: "as touching the righteousness which is in the law, blameless"; and until there is a conviction of need, there can never be a desire for a change. But God has *His* ways!

The first mark that God made on him was through his cousin, Evan Lewis. He gave Rees a sudden shock one night by asking him if he was "born again." Rees had never heard the expression. He was "as ignorant of it as Nicodemus." But he knew he was wounded and raised his defences: "What do you mean? My life is as good as yours." "That's not the point. Put it this way: Do you know you are saved?" "I am a Christian, and that's good enough for me." But though he professed to be unconvinced, his complacency was shaken. His cousin was faithful and did not let the matter drop, although it always seemed to end in fruitless argument.

But one day the arrow really found its mark. His cousin told him that when his sister was dying she had spoken to him about his own need of the Savior, and as she spoke, he had "seen Calvary." Again Rees did not know what he meant, but instinctively felt he was on holy ground, and a voice seemed to warn him not to argue any more. The impression was so strong that he decided to leave the place and seek work elsewhere, lest he should "touch the forbidden thing."

He moved about a hundred miles to Martin's Ferry, but as his cousin saw him off at the station, even his last words drove the shaft farther home: "If only you were born again I wouldn't mind your leaving, but it troubles me to see you going when you are not right with God." Rees could not forget these words. The gracious Hound of Heaven was on his trail "with unhurrying chase, and unperturbed pace," with "those strong feet that followed, followed after."

The light really began to dawn as he was reading one day an outstanding book of that time, Professor Henry Drummond's *Natural Law in the Spiritual World.* Drummond was telling how he had never thought it possible to give a definition of life, till he found one in the works of Herbert Spencer, who said that life is "correspondence with environment." A child is born with five senses and various bodily organs, and each corresponds with something in his environment: the eye sees sights, the ear hears sounds, the lungs breathe air, and so on. "While I can correspond with my environment, I have life," said Spencer; "but if something happened to me which prevented me from corresponding with my environment then I should be dead; death is failure of correspondence."

Drummond took the definition back to Adam. The Lord had told him that the day he disobeyed, he would surely die. Did he die? On Spencer's definition he died spiritually, for though he continued to have a natural life, he lost his correspondence with God and could only come back to Him by the way of sacrifice, the way of a victim killed in his stead.

On reading this, the first thought that came to Rees was, Had he correspondence with God? Could he say the Savior was as real to him as his mother? Did he know God as a daily presence in his life, or did he only think of Him in the prayer meetings? If he died, had he another environment with which to correspond? He was a part of his parents—distance didn't interfere with their fellowship, but he hadn't a relationship with God like that. Back came those words to him which his cousin had constantly been quoting: "Except a man be born again . . . he cannot enter into the Kingdom of God."

"I saw it!" said Rees. "I believed in the Savior, but one thing I knew, I wasn't *born* of Him. So far as having correspondence with the spiritual realm where the Savior lived, I was a dead man, I was outside the Kingdom, which all my good life and religion had never enabled me to enter. I was outside, though I was not a drunkard or a thief, because I had no correspondence with God."

His religious complacency was shattered. There was no great conviction of sin, but he knew there was a gulf between him and God, and á deeper concern for his eternal destiny than for any of the affairs of this life possessed his mind.

3

Meeting the Risen Lord

"Nigh and nigh draws the chase." What Rees had begun to meditate upon in theory, he soon had to face in fact. He was suddenly struck down with typhoid fever—always dangerous, but in those days often fatal, and soon he was face to face with death. In this bitter experience he was alone in lodgings and far from home, and this again was the finger of God for, he said later, "I found fear in me for the first time, and when I faced leaving this world and entering an unknown realm, pangs took hold of me, such as I had never felt before. Thank God my parents were not there to take that fear from me. Thank God that human sympathy did not blind me to eternity, for you may live in a crowd, but you meet God and face eternity alone."

He cried to the Lord not to allow him to die. The enjoyment he had had in money-making, traveling and sight-seeing was forgotten as he besought the Lord to give him eternal life. "Give me one more chance," he cried, "and I will give my life to You."

There was a vow in that cry. The Lord saw to that before He answered, and even as the cry went up Rees knew in his heart that he was not to die. From that moment he began to recover, but he was a changed man. "As I faced losing all and entering an eternal darkness, I touched real life for the first time," he said. "I had seen the world at its very best taking me down to a lost eternity, and I knew I owed my all to the God who had delivered me." From that time on, he never regarded eternity lightly, for he had faced the reality of hell—a separation from God for ever.

As he recovered, the gravity of his recent experience made him examine his position with renewed earnestness. He had been delivered from death, but not from the fear of death. He had always believed in the Incarnation, the Atonement, the Resurrection; they were the most precious truths in his life. Why then were they not real to him? If Christ had conquered death, why was he afraid of it? Those who have heard him tell of this period in his life will never forget how he rang out the answer to these questions: "I found that I had only an historical Christ and not a personal Savior who could take me to the other side."

For five months he searched daily for the way to God. He said he would gladly have spent every penny, and gone from one end of the vast country to the other, if he could only find a man to show him the way to eternal life. He did go to the only one he could think of. He took the 100-mile journey back to New Castle to ask his cousin about it but, though his cousin knew the way himself, he seemed unable to make it clear to Rees.

During these months he made another move, to Connellsville, Pennsylvania. Here at last "the chase" was to end. "Halts by me that footfall: Is my gloom, after all, Shade of His hand, outstretched caressingly?" How wonderfully each restless move had only been one further stage forward in the pursuit and capture of the prey. Rees had not been long in his new home when he heard that a converted Jew, Maurice Reuben from Pittsburgh, had come to the city for a series of meetings. The first night that he went to hear him, Reuben told the story of his conversion and how the Holy Spirit had revealed Calvary to him. "I had heard preaching on Calvary scores of times before and believed it," said Rees, "but I had never seen Calvary before that night." He was being brought back to the very same point which had so struck him in his cousin's testimony.

Maurice Reuben told how he belonged to a wealthy family and had the best the world could give him, and how he had lived to make money. He was a manager of Solomon and Reuben, one of the largest stores of Pittsburgh. But the life of one of his buyers used to put him under deep conviction, until one day he said to him, "You must have been born happy." "Yes," replied the buyer, "in my second birth. I accepted the Lord Jesus Christ and was born of God. In my first birth I was no happier than you!"

Reuben was so moved by this testimony that he bought a New Testament, and there he was impressed with the fact that all those who followed Jesus were Jews: John the Baptist pointing to Him as the Lamb of God; Peter, James and John, the chief disciples; and to a Jew the Savior had said, "On this rock will I build My Church." Then he came to the story of the rich young ruler. It was a dramatic moment—a rich Jew of the twentieth century and under conviction, reading of the Savior's dealings with a rich Jew of the first century! The way that Reuben saw it was that if Jesus had told that young man to sell all to inherit eternal life, how could he, Reuben, inherit the same gift, unless on the same condition? It was his supreme test. If he became a disciple, he knew that he too stood to lose all. But it was too late to go back; he had seen it, and he must follow. As Reuben said those words, Rees echoed them in his own heart; it was too late also for him to go back.

Reuben faced it fairly and squarely and counted the cost. His wife might leave him, his brother put him out of the business, and not a single Jew follow him, but he had made up his mind; if he lost everything, he meant to do it.

Then one day on the way to the store, Reuben heard a voice repeating to him the words of John 14:6: "I am the way, the truth, and the life: no man cometh unto the Father but by Me." The truth flashed upon him—he accepted Christ and entered into life that moment. He then told his brother and others. According to his father's will he was to forfeit every penny if he changed his religion, but his brother offered to give him £70,000—his share of the business—if he would cross

U.S.A and retire in Montana. But Reuben replied, "I have had the light in Pittsburgh, and I am going to witness in Pittsburgh."

Late that Saturday night detectives came and took him to the police station. On Monday two doctors visited his cell and asked him about the voice he had heard. "Do they question my sanity?" he thought.

Two hours later warders came from the asylum and took him to a room where there were twenty-nine mentally deranged people. The bitterness of his position overcame him. He had victory in the lock-up, but this seemed more than he could bear. He fell on his knees by his bed and poured out his heart to the Lord. He did not know how long he was there, but he seemed to lose himself, and a vision of Calvary appeared to him. He said he witnessed every stage of the crucifixion. He forgot his own sufferings in the sufferings of the Savior, and as he gazed on the cross, the Master Himself said to him, "And must I bear the cross alone, and all the world go free?" From a broken heart Reuben answered, "No. There's a cross for everyone, and there's a cross for me."

From that hour he was a new man. Instead of complaining at being in the asylum, he began to pray for the other twenty-nine, and to the Savior he said, "Let me suffer for You. Whatever You allow me to go through, I will never complain again."

Two weeks later, Reuben's brother came to see him, and reproached him for his folly in getting himself into such a place. "Why don't you be wise?" he said. "Get out of here and go to Montana." "Does that offer still stand? Then it is not a medical condition but something else that is keeping me here!" said Reuben with all the keenness of his logical mind.

Some Christian friends he was in touch with caused inquiries to be set on foot. In six weeks his release was procured. It became a court case, and the test was on "the voice."

The judge called the doctor and asked why this man had been certified as insane. "Because he heard a voice," said the doctor. "Didn't the Apostle Paul hear a voice?" countered the judge, who was a Christian man. "This is a disgrace to the American flag," and he told Reuben to prosecute anyone who had anything to do with it.

"I shall never prosecute anyone," answered Reuben, "but I will do one thing—I will pray for them." He crossed the court and offered his hand to his brother, but he turned his back on him. He went to his wife, but she did the same. But what a victory he had in his own soul!

Maurice rented a small room in Chicago, where he lived alone with the Lord and won many converts, though for two years he hardly had a square meal. A year later his wife came to hear him in a camp meeting and was converted, and for the first time he saw his little boy who had been born after his wife had left him. She was willing to make her home with him again, if only he would earn a living as other Christians did. His heart went out to his little boy, and this test was even greater than the first. Her request seemed so reasonable, but he knew that the Lord had called him from the world into this life of faith. He pleaded with the Lord, but the only reply he received was, "Back to Egypt!"

It was enough, and once more Reuben embraced the cross. He went to see his wife and child off; it was a costly experience; but as the train steamed out of the station it seemed that God poured the joy of heaven into his soul. He literally danced on the platform. He did not see his wife for another three years. Then, in another camp meeting, she too had a revelation of the cross. As a result of this she testified that, whereas before as a believer she had not been willing to share the sacrificial life of her husband, if it would be for God's glory she would now be willing to beg her bread from door to door. They were reunited and she became a wonderful co-worker with him in his ministry.

One thing that had hindered Rees Howells from coming through before was that while people said they were born again, he could not see that their lives were better than his. How then could he be convinced that they had something he had not? But he had sometimes said to the Lord, "If I ever see a person who is living the Sermon on the Mount, I will give in." Before Reuben came to the end of his story, the Lord said to Rees, "Is this your man?"

What followed in that little Methodist chapel Rees Howells tells in his own words: "As Maurice Reuben brought those sacred scenes before us, I too saw the cross. It seemed as if I spent ages at the Savior's feet, and I wept and wept. I felt as if He had died just for me. I lost myself. I had been living in the fear of death, and I saw Him taking that death for me. My parents loved me very much and, up to that time, to me there were no people like them, but they never suffered death for me. He *did* it. His love for me, as compared with theirs, was as high as the heavens above the earth, and He won my love— every bit of it. He broke me, and everything in me went right out to Him.

"Then He spoke to me and said, 'Behold, I stand at the door and knock. May I come in to you, as I came in to Reuben and took the place of wife and son and home and store and world? Will you accept me?' 'Yes,' I replied, and He came in, and that moment I changed. I was born into another world. I found myself in the Kingdom of God, and the Creator became my Father. That night I received the gift of eternal life, that gift which money cannot buy.

"When I went home, my friend who accompanied me to the meeting, but had seen nothing in it, seemed so rough to me. Everyone who was not born again seemed rough. The Savior became everything to me. He was not only the fairest among ten thousand, but fairest among millions! That love of His had always been there, but before I saw it, there was no response from me; but He had plenty of response after this. Everything of this world was rough, but everything about Him, so holy, pure and beautiful.

"I changed altogether. None of my old friends could understand what had happened. I had no fellowship with natural things. It wasn't a point of doctrine I saw; no, it was Calvary. It wasn't giving a mental assent; no, the veil was taken back, my eyes were opened, and I *saw* Him. That night I saw this world as a cursed place, and the thought came to me that I would never touch it again.

"The love of the Savior was revealed to me. You can't explain what a revelation is. I saw that the Savior and Father, before I should suffer, would rather suffer for me. No natural love is in the same world as His love. It was not merely that the Savior helped me outside Himself; no, He took my place. I saw every other love so rough in comparison. Self was the motive of it. But I could see *that* love enduring through the countless ages of eternity. When you receive the Savior, you receive the love of God. That love flooded my being, and it has flooded my being ever since.

"I saw that by His coming in to me, He would love sinners through me, as He loved me. It would not be forcing myself to love others, any more than the Savior forced Himself to love me. No person could be an enemy to me, because I had been an enemy to Him before I was reconciled. If I live in the realm where He is, I live to have mercy, and to be kind, to love others. Could the love of God in me do harm to anyone? I had left the world and its folly, and been born into that Kingdom where there is only the love of God—the most attractive life on the face of the earth."

Rees always spoke of this, his spiritual birthday, as the most outstanding day of his life. It was the day which brought his stay in America to a close. He never forgot that it was in the U.S.A. and through a Jew that he found the Savior, and that he owed a debt to God's chosen people which he was to repay in later years; but he felt that his first witness should be to his own folk, who had nurtured him in the things of God.

The thought of returning home was crystalized for him within a few days by a sharp temptation on the point of his previous weakness—the love of money. The manager of the works where he was employed had a high opinion of him, and offered him a job at $12 a day, quite a good wage for America in those days, but it would have meant more claim on his time. He told his friend that he was leaving as soon as he could, "because the manager is putting a temptation before me, and I told the Lord I would never live for money." The new life was quickly pushing out the old. As he said, he had gone out to do sightseeing, but had seen the greatest sight in the world — Calvary!

4

The Welsh Revival

Rees' return to Wales was in a strategic year. It was in 1904, the time of the great Revival, and his own recent experience just fitted him to take part it it. "In a short while the whole of the country was aflame," he said. "Every church was stirred to its depths. Strong men were in tears of penitence, and women moved with a new fervor. People were overpowered by the Spirit as on the day of Pentecost, and were counted as drunken men. In the services they were praying, singing and testifying. It was a church revival, turning Christians everywhere into witnesses: 'Certainly we cannot but speak the things which we have seen and heard.' "

The presence and power of the Holy Ghost in the church has always been a fact recognized by true believers; so it was not so much a case of asking Him to come as acknowledging His presence, and very soon realizing His power. But often they had first to pray out the hindrances to blessing: disobedience and unforgiving hearts were two sins that were constantly dealt with. On the other hand, obedience to the promptings of the Spirit and open confession of Christ brought down the blessing.

Once the first hymn was given out, the meeting conducted itself. There was no leader, but people felt an unseen control. Speakers were often interrupted by a chorus of song and prayer, but there was no sense of discord or break in the harmony. There was noise, excitement and emotion in the meetings, but it was only the effect of people being freed from bondage. When some complained, one old preacher replied that he preferred the noise of the city to the silence of the cemetery!

The Revival proved what the Holy Ghost could do through a company of believers who were of one spirit and of one mind as on the day of Pentecost. The church had seen over and over again what the Lord could do through a yielded evangelist or pastor, such as Moody or Finney, but in the Welsh Revival it was a divine power manifested through the church. The keynote was, "Bend the church and save the world."

The one aim was the saving of souls. The Savior said there is joy among the angels over one sinner that repents, and they could say there was joy in the church over the converts. The bells of heaven rang every time, and there was a shout of victory in the camp.

Under the influence of the Spirit there was an irresistible power. The feeblest ones were often clothed with a majesty that was indescribable, and their words were with unction, as they showed how the Savior was "slain for our offences and raised again for our justification." Whole congregations were melted and people were crying out in agony of soul, "What must we do to be saved?" Multitudes experienced the power of the Blood of Jesus Christ to cleanse from all sin.

But the real problem arose as the Revival proceeded and thousands were added to the churches. There were more children born than there were nurses to tend them. The establishing of the converts became the greatest need, which if not met would be the most dangerous weakness of the Revival.

As enthusiasm abated, there were bound to be many who had depended more on feelings and not yet learned to have their faith solidly based on the Word of God. The devil took advantage of this: some became cold and indifferent, and the spiritual conflict began. Those like Rees Howells, young in the Spirit though they were but at least a bit more advanced than the converts in the Revival, were needed to be intercessors and teachers, to take the burden of the new-born babes, and to pray and lead them on.

But these new intercessors soon began to find how mighty is the enemy of souls, and that a conflict not against flesh and blood but against the rulers of the darkness of this world cannot be fought with carnal weapons. They needed what they themselves had not yet received: the enduement of the Holy Ghost for service. As Rees Howells said later: "The intercession of the Holy Ghost for the saints in this present evil world must be made through believers filled with the Holy Ghost" (Rom. 8:26,27).

It was this that brought him and others to feel their need of the fullness. Nothing had been lacking in the joy and satisfaction which Rees had found in the Savior for his own personal life, but he did not know the secret of power for service.

"Many blamed the young converts for backsliding," he said, "but we blamed ourselves, because we were not in a position to pray them through to victory. Oh, the tragedy, to be helpless in front of the enemy when he was sifting young converts like wheat!

"In Isaiah 59 we read that God saw there was no man, and wondered that there was no intercessor, and this was just our case. Many of us felt the need of being 'endued with power from on High.' We were in the same position as those disciples whom the Lord told to tarry until they were endued. The record goes on to say that 'they worshipped Him and returned to Jerusalem with great joy.' They had the joy before they had the power, so joy was no proof of that enduement of the Spirit. We had that same joy in the Revival, in the knowledge of a risen Christ and the assurance of eternal life— unspeakable joy—but at the same time we felt the lack of power for service."

5

The Holy Spirit Takes Possession

On his return from America, Rees had settled down again in the old family home, where he had received a great welcome. Instead of returning to the tin mill like several of his brothers, however, he now found employment in a neighboring mine about a mile away in the valley, working underground at the coal-face—the hardest job of all.

His spare time was spent in the activities of the Revival, but the sense of spiritual need was growing among the workers, and in 1906 a large party decided to spend their summer holiday-week seeking the Lord in a special way at the Llandrindod Wells Convention, the counterpart in Wales of the English Keswick Convention for the deepening of spiritual life. For Rees Howells this was to be, after his new birth, the most revolutionary event in his life.

Shortly before they were due to go, Rees was in a meeting in Brynamman, where a young woman read Romans 8:26-30. She could only read very slowly, which gave time for each word to sink in: "Predestinated . . . justified . . . glorified." As Rees listened, he said to himself, "I know I am predestinated according to the foreknowledge of God, and justified—but am I glorified?" That puzzled him and the question was constantly in his mind: What does it mean to be glorified?

Two days later in the train on the way to Llandrindod with this thought still before him, a voice spoke to him: "When you return, you will be a new man." "But I *am* a new man," he protested. "No," came the answer, "you are a child." The others in the carriage were singing the newest song of the Revival, *The Glory Song*, but Rees never heard it. Instead, he kept pacing the corridor with that voice ringing in his ears: "You will be a new man."

On the first morning of the Convention the preacher—who was perhaps the greatest expositor on "the life in the Spirit" that Keswick has produced, the Rev. Evan Hopkins—spoke on Ephesians 2:1-6: "You hath He quickened . . . and hath raised us up . . . and made us sit together in heavenly places in Christ Jesus." He pointed out that it was the Risen Lord who had appeared to the disciples after the resurrection; but when the Holy Ghost came down He revealed the Exalted Savior at the right hand of the Father. Mr. Hopkins then asked the question, "Have you been quickened by Christ? Have you been raised up to sit with Him in heavenly places?"

In his heart Rees answered, "Yes, I know I have been quickened, but I have not been raised up with Christ to that place of power," and the moment he said that, he saw the Glorified Lord. "As really as I had seen the Crucified Christ and the Risen Christ, I saw the Glorified Christ, and the same voice I had heard in the train said to me, 'Would you like to sit there with Him? There is a place for you.' I saw myself raised up with Him. I knew now what it meant to be 'glorified.' I saw Him as John did in Patmos, and I was dazzled like the Apostle Paul. When He reveals a thing, it is exactly as it is; it is not imagination. All that night I was in the presence of God and my glorified Savior. There is nothing in nature refined enough to describe it. I saw men as trees walking."

The next morning Mr. Hopkins spoke about the Holy Spirit. He made it plain that He is a Person, with all the faculties of a Person, exactly like the Savior. He has intelligence, love and a will of His own; and as a Person, before He comes to live in a man, He must be given full possession of his body.

"As he spoke," Rees said, "the Holy Ghost appeared to me and I knew him to be the One who had spoken to me the day before and shown me that place of splendor and glory into which natural eyes can never look. It never dawned on me before that the Holy Ghost was a Person exactly like the Savior, and that He must come and dwell in flesh and blood. In fact, the Church knows more about the Savior, who was only on the earth thirty-three years, than about the Holy Ghost who has been here two thousand years. I had only thought of Him as an Influence coming on meetings, and that was what most of us in the Revival thought. I had never seen that He must live in bodies, as the Savior lived in His on earth.''

The meeting with the Holy Ghost was just as real to Rees Howells as his meeting with the Savior those years before. ''I saw Him as a Person apart from flesh and blood, and He said to me, 'As the Savior had a body, so I dwell in the cleansed temple of the believer. I am a Person. I am God, and I am come to ask you to give your body to Me that I may work through it. I need a body for My temple (1 Cor. 6:19), but it must belong to Me without reserve, for two persons with different wills can never live in the same body. Will you give me yours? (Rom. 12:1). But if I come in, I come as God, and you must go out (Col. 3:2,3). I shall not mix Myself with your self.'

''He made it very plain that He would never share my life. I saw the honor He gave me in offering to indwell me, but there were many things very dear to me, and I knew He wouldn't keep one of them. The change He would make was very clear. It meant every bit of my fallen nature was to go to the cross, and He would bring in His own life and His own nature.''

It was unconditional surrender. From the meeting Rees went out into a field where he cried his heart out because, as he said, ''I had received a sentence of death, as really as a prisoner in the dock. I had lived in my body for twenty-six years, and could I easily give it up? Who could give his life up to another in an hour? Why does a man struggle when death comes, if it is easy to die? I knew that the only place fit for the old nature was on the cross. Paul makes that very plain in Romans 6. But once this is done in reality, it is done for ever. I could not run into this.

"I intended to do it, but oh, the cost! I wept for days. I lost seven pounds in weight, just because I saw what He was offering me. How I wished I had never seen it! One thing He reminded of was that He had only come to take what I had already promised the Savior, not in part, but the whole.

"Since He died for me, I had died in Him, and I knew that the new life was His and not mine. That had been clear in my mind for three years; so He had only come to take what was His own. I saw that only the Holy Ghost in me could live like the Savior. Everything He told me appealed to me; it was only a question of the loss there would be in doing it. I didn't give my answer in a moment, and He didn't want me to."

It took five days to make the decision, days which were spent alone with God. "Like Isaiah, I saw the holiness of God," he said, "and seeing Him, I saw my own corrupt nature. It wasn't sins that I saw, but nature touched by the Fall. I was corrupt to the core. I knew I had to be cleansed; I saw there was as much difference between the Holy Ghost and myself as between light and darkness.

"Nothing is more real to me than the process I went through for that whole week," he continued. "The Holy Spirit went on dealing with me, exposing the root of my nature which was self, and you can only get out of a thing what is in its root. Sin was canceled, and it wasn't sin He was dealing with; it was self—that thing which came from the Fall.

"He was not going to take any superficial surrender. He put His finger on each part of my self-life, and I had to decide in cold blood. He could never take a thing away until I gave my consent. Then the moment I gave it, some purging took place (Isaiah 6:5-7), and I could never touch that thing again. It was not *saying* I was purged and the thing still having a hold on me: no, it was a breaking, and the Holy Ghost taking control. Day by day the dealing went on. He was coming in as God, and I had lived as a man, and 'what is permissible to an ordinary man,' He told me, 'will not be permissible to you.' "

This "Llandrindod experience" was the crisis, which was

followed by the process of sanctification (see Mr. Howells' own comment on p. 95) during which the Holy Spirit, on the basis of his initial surrender, step by step replaced the self-nature with His own divine nature (2 Peter 1:4). First there was the love of money, that "root of evil" which had formerly taken Rees to America. The Lord told him that He would take out of his nature all taste for money and any ambition for the ownership of money. "I had to consider what that meant," Rees said. "Money would be no more to me than it was to John the Baptist or to the Savior. To an extent this was dealt with in my new birth, but now the Holy Ghost was getting at the root." The dealings on that lasted a whole day, and by the evening his "attitude towards money had entirely changed."

Then there was the fact that he would never have the right to a choice in making a home. "I saw I could never give my life to another person, to live to that one alone. Could the Savior have given His life and attention to one person, instead of to a lost world? Neither could the Holy Ghost. He took plenty of time to show me exactly what it would mean: the life He would live would be for the world. Was I willing for that?"

Among other things that were dealt with was ambition. How could he have any if the Holy Ghost came in? The way the Lord showed it to him was like this: Supposing he had a mission in a town and another mission opened in the same place; if there was jealousy between the two, and it was better for the town only to have one, then it would be his which would have to go. Or suppose that he and another man should apply for the same job; he would have to let the other have it. Or if he were earning 12s. a day, and another man with a family was earning much less, the Spirit could tell him to give his job to that man. He saw the Holy Ghost in ways like that taking the place of the other, and suffering instead of him. Yes, he was willing for that.

On the fifth day his reputation was touched. As he was thinking of men of the Bible who were full of the Holy Ghost, and particularly John the Baptist, the Lord said to him, "Then I may live through you the kind of life I lived through him." A

Nazarite clothed in camel's hair, living in a desert! Even in this, or what might be its modern equivalent, a real decision had to be made. "If I live My life in you, and that is the kind of life I choose, you can't stop Me," was the Lord's word on it. As the Savior was despised, he must be willing to be the same.

By Friday night each point had been faced. He knew exactly what he was offered: the choice between temporal and eternal gain. The Spirit summed the issue up for him: "On no account will I allow you to cherish a single thought of self, and the life I will live in you will be one hundred per cent for others. You will never be able to save yourself, any more than the Savior could when He was on earth. Now, are you willing?" Rees was to give a final answer.

That night a friend said to him, "If some of us come over after the meeting, will you tell us of your position in Christ?" At once the Spirit challenged him: "How can you do that? You have seen the position of the overcomers, but you have not entered in. I have been dealing with you for five days; you must give Me your decision by six o'clock tonight and remember, your will must go. On no account will I allow you to bring in a crosscurrent. Where I send you, you will go; what I say to you, you will do." It was the final battle on the will.

"I asked Him for more time," Rees continued, "but He said, 'You will not have a minute after six o'clock.' When I heard that it was exactly as if a wild beast was roused in me. 'You gave me a free will,' I answered, 'and now You force me to give it up.' 'I do not force you,' He replied, 'but for three years have you not been saying that you are not your own, and that you wanted to give your life back to the Savior as completely as He gave His for you?'

"I climbed down in a second. The way I had said it was an insult to the Trinity. 'I am sorry,' I told Him, 'I didn't mean what I said.' 'You are not forced to give up your will,' He said again, 'but at six o'clock I will take your decision. After that you will never get another chance.' It was my last offer; my last chance! I saw that Throne (Rev. 3:21) and all my future for eternity going. I said, 'Please forgive me, I *want* to do it.'

"Once more the question came, 'Are you willing?' It was ten minutes to six. I wanted to do it, but I could not. Your mind is keen when you are tested, and in a flash it came to me, 'How can self be willing to give up self?' Five to six came. I was afraid of those last five minutes. I could count the ticks of the clock. Then the Spirit spoke again. 'If you can't be willing, would you like Me to help you? Are you willing to be made willing?'

" 'Take care,' the enemy whispered. 'When a stronger person than yourself is on the other side, to be willing to be made willing is just the same as to be willing.' As I was thinking upon that point I looked at the clock. It was one minute to six. I bowed my head and said, 'Lord, I am willing.' "

Within an hour the Third Person of the Godhead had come in. He gave Rees that word in Hebrews 10:19, "Having therefore boldness to enter into the Holiest by the blood of Jesus." "Immediately," said Rees, "I was transported into another realm, within that sacred veil where the Father, the Savior and the Holy Ghost live. There I heard God speaking to me, and I have lived there ever since. When the Holy Ghost enters, He comes in to 'abide for ever.' To the Blood be the glory!

"How I adored the grace of God! It is God who goes so far as to give us repentance. It was God who helped me to give up my will. There were some things He had asked for during the week that I was able to give, because I was the master of them; but when He asked me to give up my self and my will, I found I could not—until He pulled me through."

An eyewitness tells us that no words can describe the little meeting in the house that night; the glory of God came down. Rees started the chorus: "There's power in the Blood," and they couldn't stop singing for two hours! Then from 9 p.m. to 2:30 a.m. it was "nothing but the Holy Ghost speaking things I had never dreamed of and exalting the Savior."

When he awoke next morning he said, "I realized that the Holy Ghost had come in to 'abide for ever.' The feeling I had was that 'He brought me to the banqueting house, and His banner over me was love.' It is impossible to describe the floods of joy that followed."

Rees Howells was not a person who was given to public speaking; he was naturally quiet and retiring. But when the Holy Ghost entered, He loosed his tongue and brought His own boldness in. There was a praise meeting that morning in the Convention Tent with about a thousand present, including some two hundred ministers. The first person Rees saw there was his own minister, and if anything could have stopped him speaking, it was the fact of his presence. But during the meeting Rees stood up and told them clearly and calmly that he was calling them to be witnesses that the Holy Ghost, who had entered the Apostles on the day of Pentecost, had entered him and would produce similar results. The effect was so great that during the next week, when crowds had gathered to hear messages from a famous speaker, literally hundreds came to ask Rees how the Holy Ghost had entered him. It was the first stream of those promised rivers which, as Jesus said, flow out of those in whom the Spirit dwells.

6

Loving an Outcast

When the divine owner takes possession of a property, He has a twofold objective: intense cultivation and abounding fruitfulness. But if the land is fallow ground, He can only till it acre by acre. We shall see the Owner now at work in His newly-claimed estate.

The first acre He put under fresh cultivation in Rees Howells was his prayer life. Rees had been used to praying general prayers, but if someone had asked him if he knew he was going to get an answer, he would not have known what to say. Now the Spirit told him, "The meaning of prayer is answer and of all that I give you, see that you lose nothing." He also told him that effectual praying must be guided praying, and that he was no longer to pray for all kinds of things at his own whim or fancy, but only the prayers that the Holy Ghost gave him.

Coupled with this was another important lesson, that he was never again to ask God to answer a prayer through others if He could answer it through him. That included his money. When there was a prayer for money, he must allow his own to be used. The Holy Ghost showed him that in the unsurrendered state he could spend time in asking God to supply the foreign fields and other causes, and yet not be willing for God to answer the prayer through him; and that often the Lord is "wearied with our words." All this unreality was to be put on one side, and the Scriptures obeyed in the most practical sense.

The first prayer of this kind that the Holy Ghost prayed through him was for a young man named Will Battery. He had come to the district some years before to live with his uncle, after having had meningitis which had left him in a very weak condition. In this state liquor had got a hold on him, and he had gone from bad to worse. He hadn't slept in a bed for two years, but spent his nights in the boiler room of the tin mill. He was dirty and unshaven; he wore no socks and never tied his shoe laces. The Revival had been in the district and hundreds had been converted, but no one had reached Will. It was for this man that Mr. Howells, to his own surprise, found the Holy Ghost travailing in him. Rees was to pray him through to sanity and salvation, and love him "not in word, neither in tongue; but in deed and in truth."

"It wouldn't have come to my mind to love him," he said, "but when the Holy Ghost comes in, He brings in the love of the Savior. It seemed as if I could lay down my life for this man; there was a love pouring out of me that I never knew before. Naturally speaking, he would be the *last* one with whom I would spend my spare time, and the tin mill would be the last place."

In his free hours Rees made this man his friend and spent all his Sundays with him. He had more joy, he said, seeking to win this one, than at chapel in the company of the other believers. He even walked about the village with him, although embarrassed once or twice as people turned and stared at them, but "the Lord pulled me up on it," he rejoiced.

About ten days before Christmas the Spirit asked Rees what gift he would like, as this was the first Christmas since He had come into his life. The choice Rees made was obvious: that Will Battery should have a blessing. But from that day on Battery disappeared!

"I sought him for ten evenings," Rees said, "as a mother looks for her child. I didn't yet know the ways of the Holy Ghost, and that He wanted me to trust Him."

Then the day before Christmas Battery came to look for him. "I can hear his footsteps now," said Rees reminiscing, "and oh, the sensation of it! I hadn't the faintest idea of the love of the Holy Ghost for a lost soul, until He loved one through me. What an evening we had together! The next day I had the joy of spending my first Christmas after the Holy Ghost had come in, in the tin mill with this young man, from 10 a.m. to 6 p.m. My mother gave me a basket with Christmas dinner for the two of us; but my joy was too great to eat. Battery had the lot! At 4 p.m. he asked if he could come with me to the cottage meeting. What joy I had in walking with him there! I had never asked him to go myself, for fear of embarrassing him."

But the work was not done in a few weeks or months. Stage by stage Will was lifted, until Rees was able to put him in lodgings and get him to take a job in the mine. But even then there were lapses, such as when Rees was summoned to face an angry landlady. Will Battery had gone to bed with his pit clothes on—boots included! Rees hastily told her to send the sheets to the laundry at his expense! The day came when the chapel people were amazed to see Battery sitting in the meetings respectably dressed; but it took three years for the final victory, when at last Mr. Howells was able to persuade him to go home to his mother, who was a converted woman and had prayed for him for years. "In this way," said Mr. Howells, "I started at the bottom and loved just one; and if you love one, you can love many; and if many, you can love all."

The second outstanding prayer the Holy Ghost prayed through him was for a man who went by the name of Jim Stakes, his real name being James Thomas. It was also the means by which the Holy Spirit gave Rees Howells his first lesson in "princely giving." As he said later: "Since my money now belongs to the New Tenant, the old tenant has to be impartial about the amount He gives. The New Tenant by His nature is more generous than the old one. The latter has lived so long in Egypt and later in the wilderness under the law, that he has only been used, at best, to giving the tithe; so when the New Tenant wants to give princely gifts, He first tests the reality of the surrender. If it is proved genuine, then there will be no future conflicts when large amounts are called for." The test for Rees was on Jim Stakes.

This man had been such a low character that the common saying was: What Jim Stakes would not do, the devil himself could not do! He was one of the worst drunkards, and there was a great sensation during the Revival when he went under conviction and came out for salvation in a prayer meeting. He had a houseful of children, and through his old drinking habit was in great poverty. Rees Howells had only met him once, but knew him well by repute. One morning when in prayer, quite unexpectedly this man "stood before" him.

"I had never before known such a conflict for a soul in the spiritual realm," Rees said. "For an hour it was as much as I could do to allow the Holy Ghost to pray through me. I saw the devil attacking him, and that if he could get him back it would be one of the best things he could do to counteract the work of the Revival. I saw that it was a conflict between God and the devil for a soul, and I told the Lord I would do anything, if He would keep him."

That very evening there was a man at the door to see him. Rees never had a greater surprise. It was Jim Stakes! He had come a distance of two miles because, he said, that while he was working in the mine that morning, at ten o'clock Rees Howells had "stood before" him. It was at that very hour in the morning that Jim Stakes had "stood before" Rees, and the burden of prayer had come on him!

"Are you in trouble?" Rees asked him. He was indeed. He was two years behind in his rent, and that morning the bailiffs had marked his furniture and were coming to fetch it. Two years' rent! That was a lot of money.

After a moment's hesitation Mr. Howells said, "I'll give you one year's rent—and I have a friend who, I believe, will give you the other half." He went upstairs to fetch the money, but before he reached the top, the Holy Spirit spoke to him. "Didn't you tell Me this morning that you would give *all* you had to save him? Why are you only giving him half? Did not the Savior pay *all* your debt and set you free?"

Rees Howells turned and ran down the stairs and said to the man, "I'm sorry I told you I would only give one year's rent. I am to give you two years' rent, and all you need beside. I am to deliver you in such a way that the devil can't use this situation any longer to get at you."

"The moment I said that," Mr. Howells declared later, "the joy of heaven came down. It was as if something snapped in my nature, and it became more blessed to give than to receive." The amount of the gift was £70.

Mr. Howells took him straight over that evening to see a friend and have prayer together. On the way he asked him if his wife was converted. Hadn't she seen a change in him and wasn't she glad? "Yes," Jim replied, "but she is not saved; she hasn't had the clothes to go to meetings."

As he listened, Rees Howells said he felt in the Spirit as though virtue had gone out to her, and he knew that she too would be converted. The following Sunday he went to their house and found her under conviction. The "princely gift" had broken her down, love had conquered, and the Holy Spirit led her to the foot of the cross, where she saw that a still greater debt had been paid for her, and paid with a greater price—the precious blood of Christ.

The blessing of this couple was what Rees called "the beginning of days" in the district, because cottage meetings were started in their home every Saturday and Sunday evening, led by Rees Howells and his friends. Many came to them, and some of the worst characters gave their hearts to the Lord.

In this new experience of life in the Holy Ghost, Rees had one whose fellowship meant much to him—his Uncle Dick. When Rees returned from Llandrindod not all believers, by any means, could see the need of this total surrender to the Holy Spirit, and some even opposed the idea. But God gave him one of like mind and heart in his uncle.

Of all the believers in the district it might have been thought that Uncle Dick had least need of this full surrender. For twenty-six years he had been an invalid, not able to walk more than a few yards, nor to read to himself more than a few minutes at a time. He had accepted this condition as the will of God, and spent hours daily in prayer or in having the Bible read to him by members of the family. Before the Revival, when the spiritual state in the country had been so low, he had joined with many in praying for a quickening and had greatly rejoiced when the answer came.

Yet he also knew his own need. Before the Revival, even among the most godly in the churches, few had known of eternal life as a free gift, or of assurance of forgiveness of sins. Even after the Revival the truth of the Holy Spirit as a divine Person living in the believer's body was hidden from most, including Uncle Dick. He had a longing for more power in prayer, but had never known how to get it.

Uncle Dick rejoiced in Rees' conversion and it was to him that Rees continued to look up to as his most valued spiritual guide. Naturally, he would be the first to whom Rees would go on his return from Llandrindod to tell of his new experience. But the visit was not an easy one, because the Lord had revealed to Rees that he was to offer the Holy Spirit to his uncle and, where the younger had been accustomed to being blessed through the elder, the reverse was now to be the case.

But Uncle Dick was ready. As Rees told him of the blessing and price—a complete surrender of the will with no reserve —his uncle recognized it as the Word of the Lord and the truth of the Scriptures. It took him three weeks to settle the matter. Each visit Rees made, his uncle would say, "I am sure I will be through in a few days"; and when he did come through, it was to glorious victory. He was an illustration of the fact that a man may be godly and devoted and yet still need the Holy Ghost, and find it by no means easy to make a full surrender.

From that time onwards, and for many years, the fellowship in the Spirit between uncle and nephew was very deep. It was a spiritual partnership in which Uncle Dick became Rees' chief prayer partner. He continued his prayer-work for some eight hours a day, but with this difference: up to the time when the Holy Ghost took full possession, any need that arose automatically became a subject of prayer. But from henceforward, as with Rees, it was guided praying with specific objectives, victorious travail, and definite answers.

7

A Village Untouched by the Revival

About half a mile from Jim Stakes' home there was a village without a single Christian or a single place of worship. At the time of the Revival people had started prayer meetings in the village, but they soon fell through. After Jim Stakes and his wife had been blessed, the Lord one day said to Mr. Howells, "As you had such joy in helping these two, wouldn't you like to help a whole village? But in going there, I have another lesson to teach you—you must be the first sufferer." This meant that he must be like a father who is the first to suffer in his family, or a good shepherd who will lay down his life for the sheep.

The Spirit showed him that the Savior took the sinner's place as Sin-bearer, Sickness-bearer and Burden-bearer, and that in going to the village he was to allow the Spirit to reveal the love of the Savior through him in a practical way. These people had had the best preaching in the Revival, and it had not touched them; but the Holy Spirit was taking His servant there to be the first sufferer, and everyone who was in need would have a claim on him to supply that need.

So one Sunday morning Mr. Howells, with his friend Johnny Lewis, Miss Elizabeth Hannah Jones (later to become Mrs. Howells), and other young Christian workers who had joined him, visited the village. Never before had they seen such a sight. Barrels of beer were placed out in the open and people were drinking and gambling and playing all kinds of games.

The place had been well named Hell-fire Row. But as Mr. Howells said afterwards, "I had only one thought: that the Holy Ghost was going there, and He had authority to cast out devils and forgive sins."

And so it proved in the first home he visited. The woman of the house was unwilling to disclose to her visitors that she was baking on Sunday, so she allowed her bread to get burnt in the oven. When Mr. Howells heard of this, he went back and told her he had come to pay for the damage he had done and placed a sovereign on her table!

A good deed has wings, and very soon the villagers learned that this band of young people, all workers themselves in pit or shop, were coming with something more than words. The woman opened her cottage for meetings and she and her husband, who had both been drunkards, were the first converts, the woman particularly continuing as one of the best in the village.

The Spirit made it plain to Mr. Howells that he was to "live out the Bible" to the people. As their clothes were different from his, he was to dress more plainly so as to attract no attention to himself. He had brought a gold watch back from America, as well as giving one to each of his brothers and sisters, but he was not to wear his again.

"If you are the first sufferer, don't have a thing these people can't have," the Lord said to him. Nearly everyone in the village was in need, and the Spirit reminded him of the Sermon on the Mount: "Give to him that asketh thee." "Whoever is in need has a *claim* on you," He said. "You have given Me all you have, and I tell you that it is all for the people, and they have as much right to it as you have."

The greatest break came when the Lord laid hold of the ringleader among the drunkards. For a long time Mr. Howells prayed for him and asked for a chance to get at him. This man could see the love of God expressed toward others, but he had not yet experienced it himself. The opportunity came.

There was some trouble outside the village. This man was involved and it was to be a court case. The Lord then said to

Rees Howells, "Now is your chance. Offer to settle the case for him." So he called at the man's home and asked him, "Would you be relieved if this case could be settled out of court? If the other people are willing to accept compensation, would you like me to pay it for you?"

The man was speechless. "He was every inch a man," observed Mr. Howells. "Mere words could never reach him, but when he saw the love of God like that, he was touched on a vital spot and broke down. He confessed that he had been to blame, and started to come to the meetings, and his love for one could be felt."

It wasn't long before over a dozen were converted, and regular meetings were started, including a Sunday School and a Band of Hope. So many left the public houses and turned to the Lord that the band of workers felt they must give all their time to be with them. They had five meetings a week and spent the other evenings visiting in the homes. The work of the Spirit spread far beyond this village and soon there were converts scattered through all the neighborhood. There was such power in the ministry that it used to be said, "If Rees Howells visits a home, you watch, someone will be converted there!"

Mr. Howells was earning his weekly wage at the colliery and also had some other savings, but at this rate he saw that his money would soon be finished. It was then that the Spirit showed him both a commandment and a promise. To the rich young man the Savior had given the command, "Sell all that thou hast and distribute unto the poor . . . and come, follow Me." And to those who did so follow He had promised, "There is no man that hath left house, or brethren, or lands, for My sake and the gospel's, but he shall receive an hundred-fold now in this time."

Rees saw that if he gave £1, the Savior said he was to get £100. Could this be true? If it was, he would surely look forward to the day when he would come to his extremity. But was it true? That was what captured his imagination—not the fact of being without money, but the possibility of it being replaced through the promises. Could that exchange really take place and he get the hundredfold?

The day came when he reached his last pound. The Holy Spirit then told him, "Cut the ropes and take the promises." It was a direct call to step out on God. But it is always easier to talk of such things than actually to do them. It had been much easier to give £100 out of plenty than to part with this last £1 and come to the end of his savings—for the first time in fifteen years.

"Oh, how the devil pitied me and brought such arguments!" he said. "He told me it would be a step in the dark and that if there was a convention or anything of that kind, I wouldn't be able to go unless I had £1 laid by. But the Holy Ghost showed me that if God wanted me to go anywhere, He would surely provide the means. The danger was on the other side: for if a person has money, he can go without consulting God, like Jonah, who could afford to pay his passage to run away from Him! The fact is, we can never really be bondservants until God does control our means."

So Rees took the plunge and learned the blessed truth that his extremity was indeed God's opportunity. His eyes were opened to the fact that he had a claim on God for what he could not supply himself. Just as surely as the Spirit had told him that the people of the village had a claim on his money to meet their needs, so now he saw that he had a claim on God's resources to meet his. The first week his need was for £2, and he was able to tell the Lord in his prayer that he would not have come to Him if he had had it himself.

"I was only asking the Lord to do what I would have done if I had had the money; and it was for His work. It came, and what joy I had in finding that I had finished with the limited resources of man and begun on the unlimited resources of God! The promises of God had replaced money in the bank and became equal to current coin to me. I no longer had to carry my treasure with me wherever I went because I knew where the Treasury was, and how to reach it!"

The greatest test in the village came when a strike was imminent. The last had continued for eight months, with great hardships to the work-people, and Mr. Howells realized that the next one might go on as long. With this burden weighing on him, the Lord asked him one question. Would he allow the Holy Ghost to do through him for the people of the village what he would do for his own family? The Bible had promised that bread and water would be sure. Would he make that promise to the village and give them bread and cheese, and tea and sugar? He knew the two grocers would give him credit though they would not allow any to the villagers. Would he run up to £100? It was a tremendous challenge. How could he do such a thing?

It was not till the Sunday night before the strike was due to begin that he came up to it. Then he told them in the meeting, "This strike may last nine months, but not one of you will be in need of what God has promised. There is no need for one of you to be troubled or fearful." The blessing that came down that night was so great, he said, that they had to close the meeting and go out to the open air. "It seemed that the singing ascended to heaven and the angels came down to meet us."

The next morning he happened to meet a well-known agnostic, who at once started grumbling at the uselessness of the church and railing against the mining authorities as the cause of the strike. "Well, what are you yourself going to do for the people in their sufferings?" Mr. Howells asked him; and then he told him what the Lord had made him promise the people the night before. The man was dumb. This was a Christianity against which there was no argument. Before he could recover, the newspaper boy came by with the news that the strike had been settled!

Every night for three years Rees Howells went over to that village, walking two miles each way after his day's work was over. The weather never stopped him. One night, when he arrived home soaked after crossing the bleak common in a downpour, his father remarked, "I wouldn't have walked across there tonight for £20." "Nor would I for £20!" answered Rees.

8

The Tramps

Every young servant of God has to learn to keep the body under (1 Cor. 9:27). In the early days of his training he goes through necessary disciplines. "If thy right hand offend thee, cut it off . . . ."

God began to deal with a simple appetite in Rees Howells—the love of food. It was at a time when he had a great burden for a certain convention which was being disrupted by assaults of the enemy. The Lord called him to a day of prayer and fasting, which was something new to him. Used as Rees was to a comfortable home and four good meals a day, it came as a shock to realize that it meant no dinner, and he was agitating about it. And would it only happen once? Supposing God asked him to do it every day!

When midday came he was on his knees in his bedroom, but there was no prayer that next hour. "I didn't know such a lust was in me," he said afterwards. "My agitation was the proof of the grip it had on me. If the thing had no power over me, why did I argue about it?"

At one o'clock his mother called him, and he told her he wasn't taking lunch. But she called again, as a mother would, and urged, "It won't take you long to have it." The goodly aroma from downstairs was too much for him, and down he came.

But after the meal, when he returned to his room, he couldn't get back into the presence of God. He came face to face with disobedience to the Holy Ghost. "I felt I was like the man in the garden of Eden," he said. "I went up the mountain and walked miles, cursing that 'old man' within me. I felt that if God were to take lunch from me to the end of my days, He would be justified in doing it. To some people there might seem nothing in it, but once you are God's channel, on no account can you disobey Him or bring in your own ideas. I wept many tears, and it almost seemed as if He would never allow me to come back into His presence, till He said, 'I will forgive you, but you are not to go unpunished. You hold up your hands while you pray from 6 to 9 o'clock' " (Ex. 17:11,12; 1 Tim. 2:8).

The closer a person is to God, the more terrible is the least sin seen to be.

He didn't take dinner for many days after that, but spent the hour with God. As he said later, "The moment I got victory in it, it wasn't a very big thing to do; it was merely a stepping-stone to His next call to me. It is while you still want a thing that you can't get your mind off it. When you have risen above it, He may give it back to you; but then you are out of its grip."

Not long after this, and only a few months after he had started the ministry in the village, the Lord gave him a further commission, for which these lessons were an obvious preparation. He laid on him the burden of the tramps—the many men who were to be found in that district wandering homeless and jobless from place to place. They were to give a chance to every tramp that came to the mission. It was to be a practical lesson of what divine love is towards an undeserving sinner.

The Spirit made plain what they were to do: to give each man a new suit of clothes, find him lodgings and work, and pay his board until he drew his first pay. "We were called to put Isaiah 58 into practice," said Mr. Howells. " 'Deal thy bread to the hungry . . . bring the poor that are cast out to thy house; and when thou seest the naked, cover him.' In our first love, we had blamed everyone who did not believe that the Bible was literally true; the Spirit now compelled us to put our own belief into practice! The Sermon on the Mount stated the laws of the Kingdom, and we were to act on them to the hilt: 'If any man take away thy coat, let him have thy cloak also . . . . Give to him that asketh thee . . . . Love your enemies . . . .'

"I soon found out also that the aim of the Spirit in this was to bring me to that grade in life where I would love the unlovely ones. My self-nature and natural love had to be changed for the divine nature and love before I could love a tramp as my own brother. Helping the people of the village was easy compared with helping the tramps, for they were people who usually would not help themselves, and often did not appreciate the help of others. But I was to act towards each exactly as I would if he were my own brother."

The very day of this new commission they saw a tramp in their meeting for the first time. He had been on the road for months, without work or lodgings, and had heard the singing in the mission. He was overcome with the reception he was given. One of the believers provided him with lodgings and found him work. In two days another came. "News of charity is like wireless," Mr. Howells said, "carried far and wide in no time, and a greater number came than we had bargained for. We were not allowed to stop them; if they came of their own accord, we did not dare to turn them away. I didn't call them tramps—I preferred the name the Savior used and called them prodigals—and I learned, according to 1 John 4:20, that you don't love the Savior one bit more than you love the least one He died for."

In all this the Spirit was leading His servant more and more into the secret of intercession—the identification of the intercessor with the ones for whom he prays. He had called him to associate with Will Battery, which had touched his pride. He had made him responsible for the debts of Jim Stakes, which had touched his pocket. Now He called him to share in the physical sufferings of the destitute, which would touch his body. He was to learn a little how to feel as they felt and sit where they sat. Tramps did not have the plentiful food that other people have, and God called him to come down to their level. The Government lodging houses provided two meals a day for tramps, and the Lord told Rees Howells to live in the same way, on two meals of bread and cheese and soup. The midday fasts had been a preparation for this.

The difficulty was, naturally, in his own home where his mother was most unwilling to let him live like that, while doing the heavy work of a miner. However, he insisted, backing his arguments by reference to the four young men in Babylon who, after their days of abstinence, looked "fairer and fatter" than the rest. His mother had to consent, although the story goes that with motherly ingenuity she put all the nourishment she could into the evening soup!

He had one meal at 6:30 in the morning and the other at 5:30 in the evening, after his day's work in the pit, and before he started for the village. It was a battle at first, both physically and mentally, eating at the same table with others, and having different food. "There was great suspicion about where this new thing would end," he said, "and what my object was in doing it. Neither they nor myself had ever seen a man called to fasting, and they thought 'the experiment' would soon come to an end. But in less than a fortnight the Lord had so changed my appetites that I preferred those two meals a day to the four I used to have. That craving for food was taken out of me, and through the whole period my health was better than anyone else's. I never had a shade of headache, and my body was fit as could be." He lived like that for two and a half years.

Supplying the needs of the tramps soon absorbed all the earnings of the little group at the mission and they were forced on still farther into a life of faith. The parable of the friend at midnight was very real to them in those days, the only difference being that he only went once to disturb his friend and they were forced to go almost every night! They proved, said Mr. Howells, what the Rev. Evan Hopkins used to teach of the three positions: struggling, clinging, and resting.

The illustration Mr. Hopkins used was of a shipwreck, when people are thrown into the sea. In the *struggling* position they are in the water, fighting against the waves, and are in need of help themselves. In the *clinging* position they are holding on to the boat—they are quite safe themselves, but cannot help anyone else because both their hands are occupied. In the *resting* position they are sitting in the boat with both hands free to help others. The place of deliverance was always when they got to the resting faith.

"When we first started to help them," Rees said, "we were afraid too many would come in the same fortnight, and that we could not provide for them; and while there was fear there was inward struggle. We soon found out that we *could not* provide, and that was just the place to which the Lord wanted us to come. Then we had to find out that God could, if we would trust Him. The Holy Ghost allowed us to be failures once or twice, so we left off struggling and trying to do it ourselves. We clung to God's promises, pleading with Him to come to our rescue, and He never failed us.

"After many hard experiences we found the resting place. We became like waiters serving in a restaurant: it wasn't our business whether ten, fifteen or twenty would come, we knew the Manager would not fail to provide what was needed. We told the Lord to send as many as He liked!

"We paid the grocer's bill every two weeks, when we got together and emptied our pockets. On one occasion, when we knew the bill was heavy, one sick brother who was not earning said, 'I am ashamed that I have only got 4½d. Shall I put that in?' The answer was, 'Yes. It will be like the widow's mite.' We entered the store, were given the bill, and found that the 4½d. made up the money needed to the penny! We learned that night not to despise the little gifts. Over and over again we found the money coming to the needed penny, and that gave us more joy than if we had had £10 over."

In three months many of these men were helped; each received a new suit of clothes, was found work, and put in good lodgings. Some received eternal life. One evening sixteen of them were in the meeting, well dressed, and singing from their hearts, "It is well with my soul." A brother sitting next to

Mr. Howells whispered, "Yes, and wit their bodies too!"

But only those who have done such work can know its real cost. There were occasions when the same tramp came back after he had been given a new suit of clothes. He had sold it, and came for another! There was an elderly woman who had fallen very low through drink and would wander in the streets "seeing things." They found her a lodging, but when she fell ill with pneumonia neither her son nor her daughter would nurse her. Mr. Howells himself was with her one whole night, and on his return home in the morning even his mother rebuked him for "being up all night looking after that old sinner." Rees had to remind her that the Father received us all back "with nothing but our filthy rags."

In another instance he found a house for a family of tramps, and got the husband work. When another family came for help he asked the first ones to share their house with them, as it was large enough. "What! Take tramps into our home!" was the answer he received. Without a word he turned away and sought another place for them.

"After many months in this school of faith," said Rees, "the Holy Ghost put such love in our hearts towards these people that we would rather be without ourselves than allow them to be in want. We became fathers to them. There were many disappointments; but some were allowed to disappoint us because it was part of our training. Some did not appreciate the kindness, but have often grieved the Holy Ghost and trampled under foot the Blood of the Covenant. We had plenty of facts with which to silence the critics, who were many."

Rees' final test with the tramps was in his own home. Anything in the way of cast-off clothing he had already been accustomed to take over to the village. Indeed, his mother made a joke of the fact that whereas they used to have a box-room full of worn garments, after a while she couldn't find a bit of cloth with which to patch anything! But the test became more severe when the tramps began to come to the house.

The Lord had told Rees that he was not to take a different place for himself at home from that which was given to the tramps. "I knew that to turn them out would be to turn the Savior out," he said, "and I could see a test coming. It might mean I would have to make a stand and walk out." Then one night it came to a head.

Some members of the family said they would leave the home if things went on like that. Every time they came home from work these tramps were there who always sat in their father's chair and did not get up when he entered. Also, they said that they would not be responsible if anything happened to their mother when they were all out.

"It was one of the worst tests in my life," said Rees, "seeing the possibility of my father's home being broken up. But my father was given great wisdom in the answer he made. He said to the others, 'If I stop the tramps, are you willing for me to stop *your* friends coming? We all bring our friends home, and if Rees has sunk so low as to have only tramps for his friends, they must be free to come too.' The victory was won, and the strange part was that after that not another tramp came to the house."

9

Binding the Strong Man

One night, when Rees Howells and his friends were returning from the village, they passed a group of women who never came to the meetings. They could tell by their voices that they had been drinking. One of the party exclaimed, "Where is the power to change *these* people?" It was a challenge, and Rees Howells took it. There and then the Spirit gave it to him that he was to pick out the ringleader of those women, who was a notorious character and a confirmed drunkard, and pray her into the Kingdom by Christmas Day!

This was something new! He had seen many drunkards converted, but the Lord had worked through his personal contacts with them; in this case, however, he had no connection with the woman and the Lord told him that he was to use no personal influence, but to reach her by way of the Throne. It would be a real test of strength. Could the Holy Spirit through him use the power of the atonement to break the devil's dominion in her life and fulfill the Savior's word in Matthew 12:29, about binding the strong man and stealing his goods? He saw that if he could get this one visible proof of the devil's defeat, the Holy Ghost could apply the victory through him on a large scale.

To do this, the Spirit gave him John 15:7: "If ye abide in Me, and My words abide in you, ye shall ask what ye will and it shall be done unto you." It would all depend on his abiding.

As this "abiding" was to take such a central place in his

future life of intercession, it is important to see what the Holy Spirit taught Mr. Howells about it. This key text, John 15:7, makes it plain that the promise is unlimited, but its fulfillment depends on the abiding. That is why in all cases of intercession, Mr. Howells constantly spoke of guarding his "place of abiding."

The Scriptural key to abiding is in 1 John 2:6, "He that saith he abideth in Him ought himself also to walk, even as He walked." In other words, it meant being willing for the Holy Spirit to live through him the life the Savior would have lived if He had been in his place.

The way Mr. Howells maintained this abiding was by spending a set time of waiting upon God every day during the period in which the intercession lasted. The Holy Spirit would then speak to him through the Word, revealing any standard that he was to come up to, particularly in "the laws of the Kingdom"—the Sermon on the Mount. Any command the Spirit gave him, he must fulfill because the way of abiding is the keeping of His commandments (John 15:10). The Spirit would also search his heart and throw light on his daily life, revealing any motives or actions that needed confession and cleansing in the Blood.

But the Spirit's dealings were not so much with outward shortcomings as with the self-nature out of which they sprang. Any transgression was never to be repeated, but specific obedience on that point would be called for until radical inward change was effected. He was "purified . . . in obeying the truth through the Spirit" (1 Peter 1:22). He could never come into God's presence unless he had obeyed all that had been given him on the previous day.

The necessity for abiding is seen in that same chapter—John 15. The life is in the Vine. As the branch remains united to it by abiding in it, that life of the Vine produces the fruit through the branch. In other words, the power is in *Christ*. As the intercessor remains united to Him by abiding in Him, His power operates through the intercessor and accomplishes what needs to be done.

As Mr. Howells would continue in this place of abiding day by day he would be increasingly conscious that the Spirit was engaging the enemy in battle and overcoming him, until finally he would become fully assured of the victory. The Spirit would then tell him that the intercession was finished, the position gained, and he would await the visible deliverance in praise and faith.

There are degrees and stages in abiding. The deeper the oneness, the more the power of the risen life of Christ can operate through the channel, and new positions of spiritual authority be gained. Rees Howells' abiding was always according to the light given up to that time. In that sense abiding in a particular period could be called "perfect," and the victory claimed although there would still be further ways in which he was to become more like the Savior.

During the first week of the abiding, the Lord spoke to him nightly on many things. "He began to deal with my nature," he said, "and show me things I never dreamed were there, getting deep down to my motives. It was a daily dying. Over and over again I thought: Is it possible to retreat?"

But with obedience came cleansing, until by the second week, he said, "I had become more used to my position, and could see the Holy Ghost binding the devil. I soon realized I was not fighting against flesh and blood, but 'against wicked spirits in heavenly places.' "

The weeks that followed, as he "gave prompt obedience to the Holy Spirit in all things," were times of wonderful fellowship, until by the end of the sixth week the Spirit told him the abiding was complete and the victory assured. "I was abiding now without being called to abide, walking in the position, and the Lord told me that I could now expect to see this woman make a move."

That very night, with a thrill in his soul, Rees saw her in the open air meeting for the first time, and he told the devil, "Now I know that the Holy Ghost is stronger than you; you have been brought to nought on Calvary."

He took no steps to influence the woman in any way, but

soon she began to come to the cottage meetings. A great number of people became onlookers as they had heard of the prayer. It was now a case of praising before the victory, and in the remaining weeks before Christmas the Holy Spirit did not allow him to pray for her. "It was a conflict with not praying," he said, "as the adversary pressed on us the need of prayer; but it would have been a prayer of doubt." During that time there was no outward sign of repentance in the woman.

Christmas morning came, and the word he had was, *Go up and possess it.* "I had a chance of experiencing what men like Moses went through in telling a thing beforehand," he said. "Not a single doubt came to my mind that day, and how strong I was! I was praising the Lord all day. I would not look at my Christmas cards or presents, for this was my Christmas gift!"

When the time for the meeting came, the woman was there, but a lot of people had brought their children; there was plenty of noise, and in no sense the kind of atmosphere which would influence a person to repent. But in the middle of the meeting "down she went on her knees and cried to God for mercy. It was a victory beyond value, and she is standing today."

Within a short time Rees Howells was able to prove again that a great secret had been learned. A manager of a works in the neighborhood, although boasting that he had never been on his knees in prayer, had been touched by what had been done for the tramps, and gave them jobs in his factory. He used to say to any of them that came to him, "You are living on the backs of those young men, are you? You start here tomorrow!"

The manager's wife had been blessed, so it came to the band of young workers to pray him through to salvation. As they waited on God, the question arose, How could they get at him? Finally they were definitely led to pray that he would invite them to his home. He did—the following Sunday!—although, to avoid frightening him, they didn't say anything about their prayer, but just sang hymns and had a happy time together.

They were invited again for tea, and this time he was more at ease. He then asked them to come the following Thursday to hold a meeting. "As soon as we left his house that night," said Mr. Howells, "the Holy Ghost told me to apply the gained position of intercession. We joined together in a ring and prayed, 'Now, Lord, the devil has been bound; don't allow this man to escape, don't give him a second chance.' The Lord then told us to abide until next Thursday and we would get the victory."

When the Thursday evening came, four of them were walking up to the village. As they passed a group of houses, the Spirit said to Mr. Howells, without any previous warning, "Go to that house and knock at the door." How could he do such a thing? He didn't even know anyone in that row of houses. How could he knock at a strange door without any known reason, or even a tract to give?

The guidance seemed so strange that he could not bring himself to act on it. He passed the house and went on a few hundred yards when the Lord's hand came on him and He told him emphatically that he was not to go to the meeting unless he went via that house. He knew there was no escaping now, so he turned back and took one of his friends with him.

When they knocked at the door, a little girl opened it and, without any questions, invited them in. There they found a woman lying in bed in the last stages of tuberculosis. When Mr. Howells told her who they were, she raised both her hands and exclaimed, "God has answered my prayer! I have been asking Him all this day to send you here!"

The night before, her friends had thought she was dying and had sent for the minister. He had brought the sacrament, but she refused to take it, because she hadn't peace. Someone had told her of their work in the mission, and it came to her that the ones who had brought such blessing there could surely help her to find peace. The woman had been a church member for years! but had no assurance of salvation, and as she was sinking, the fear of death had taken hold of her. They were able to point her to Calvary and she accepted Christ that night.

As she received assurance and became free, it was "joy fathomless as the sea." Every Thursday evening after that they had a meeting in her house. She never ceased to thank them until she passed peacefully away into the presence of the King.

Rees and the others were late in getting to the meeting in the home of the works manager that night, but the Lord did more in a few minutes through their obedience than might have been done in hours without it. While they were telling what had happened to the dying woman, the manager went down on his knees as if he had been shot, pulling his chair on top of him, and pleaded with God to have mercy on him. "It was an opened heaven," said Rees Howells, "and we joined the angels in their joy over a sinner that had repented."

10

A Branch in the Vine

There was to be a special meeting one night in the village and a friend of Rees Howells was to give the address. The two had arranged to walk over to the village together, but when it was time to start, the special speaker sent word that he could not come. On hearing this, Rees was greatly upset—and he realized why. He had not been carrying a burden for the meeting that day as he usually did; he had been depending more on his friend than on the Holy Spirit. He soon found also that the Presence which usually accompanied him on the night journey to the village was withdrawn, and the Spirit was grieved. He walked about half way with a heavy heart until he could bear it no longer. "Please forgive me," he said to the Lord. "I promise that it will never happen again. If You will only come and give victory in this meeting, then I vow like Jephthah that on my return tonight, I will give You whatever You ask."

There was a great blessing in the meeting and, walking home, as he came to the place of his vow, he asked the Lord what He would have of him. The answer was unexpected. "After tonight," the Lord said, "I want you to be a steward, and not an owner. Will you give up all claim on your money to Me?"

Rees did not understand this. Was not his money already the Lord's? The Lord then showed him his position. He had previously faced the fact that he could not ask God to meet a need if he could supply it himself. So all his money had actually been spent in the Lord's work. But it was still his money and he had the joy of giving it, and the right to give or withhold.

"In the future, as a steward," the Lord said, "you will not have the right even to give without My permission. And not a penny of My money will be spent except on essentials." Explaining what He meant by this, the Lord asked him, "If you had a family of children who were without food or clothing, would you spend a penny on a daily paper, or on any non-essential?" "No." "Well, the world is My parish, and while there is one person needing the necessities of life you will not spend a penny on anything else."

He faced what it would mean to lose that joy of giving, and the bondage he would be in for the rest of his days. But he had come before God to pay his vow. So, turning from the path, he knelt on the grass at the side of the road and, as there was no one else present, he called the stars and the cloud of witnesses to record that from that night on he was only a channel.

As he walked on, the enemy whispered, "Do you know what you have done? You are worse off than a man in Swansea jail. He gets a little which he can spend when he comes out, but you will never have a penny." "Yes," answered Rees, "but remember this—I did it *by choice*." The moment he said that, "it seemed as if the whole heavens were illuminated," and the Holy Spirit said to him, "Let Me tell you what you have done. Tonight I have grafted you into the Vine, and all the sap can flow through you. You are a branch in the Savior. The branch gets nothing—it is the needy that get the fruit. But after tonight, from this place of abiding, whatever the Father wants to pour out to the world through you, He can do so. 'Herein is My Father glorified, that ye bear much fruit.' Because you have done this for Me, you are no longer a servant, but I have called you a friend." A friend of the Trinity! It was a personal revelation of the Savior's words in John 15, and for days, Rees said, the joy and realization of it overcame him.

For the next eighteen months he never spent a penny except on necessities; and it was through that period that he had all sense of ownership of money taken out of him. The real test, as it often is, was on a very fine point, and did not come for four months. It was a matter of one penny and, as he remarked, "it shows how keenly the Husbandman watches the branch."

At the last Llandrindod Convention he had met a gentleman from London, Mr. John Gosset, of whom we are to hear more. This friend had asked for his address, and then at Christmas sent him two books and a card. The conflict came over the desire to send a New Year's card back to him with a letter of thanks. He said, "I naturally wanted to return the compliment. I thought, 'It will only cost me a penny'; but the Holy Ghost made plain that what mattered was not the amount but the principle, and the obedience in maintaining the position. A New Year's card was not a necessity of life!" So he wrote to Mr. Gosset thanking him for the books, at the same time giving him the reason for not sending a card. After the letter had been posted, an attack came from the accuser of the brethren: "Now you have insulted your friend! You are suggesting that he is misusing his money." However, the young steward was able to trust his Master that He would not let the enemy convey a false impression, which was not intended.

Two weeks later they were praying for £2 and had to get it on a certain day. That very morning a letter came from London. It was from Mr. Gosset, and when Rees Howells opened it, the first thing he found was £2 enclosed. The letter ran: "Received your letter, and the blessing I got through it was of more value to me than all the Christmas and New Year cards put together. Every Sunday I visit the Westminster hospital, so last Sunday your letter was my sermon to the patients: A position gained through grace. Whenever you need money for your work, if you will only let me know, it will be my joy to share in it." That, of course, Mr. Howells would never do; his needs were to be made known only by way of the Throne. "But," he added, "I found it quite easy to reach this gentleman in that way! He became a great friend and was often used by the Lord to answer our prayers."

In commenting later on this radical dealing of the Spirit with him, Mr. Howells said: "I finished with ownership once for all. I became as dead to money as to the stones on the road. It was a great joy in those days to think that the Savior had made me a branch—just a channel through which His own resurrection life could flow to the needy world. There is no closer relationship than between a branch and the Vine.

"But one thing the Husbandman cannot do is to graft the old life into the Vine. Self can never abide in the Savior—not one atom of it. Before you can be grafted into the Vine, you must be cut off from the old life. That had been going on and there were many stages in my life before this came. Without His new life, all our activity and work is, in the sight of God, as nothing. Yet the Vine can't do anything without the branch. All the sap of the Tree is running through the branch. And when this new life flows through us, every bit of us tingles with it, even our very body itself. If the Vine has joy, the branch has the same joy, and the needy get the fruit."

In future years Rees Howells was to handle the Lord's money by the thousands of pounds and, as he later said, "He has never questioned me on anything I spent." For such a stewardship, with never again a claim to ownership, the experience of that night and the eighteen months' obedience which followed formed the essential preparation.

11

The Tubercular Woman

The first case of severe illness among the converts in the village brought a new challenge to Mr. Howells. It was the woman with the burnt bread. She developed tuberculosis. The doctor had given her up and she was expected to die. Then one evening she revived remarkably and announced to her friends that the Great Physician had told her she was to be healed.

In the morning she sent for Mr. Howells and questioned him as to whether the Lord had revealed anything to him. He said He had not, for up to that time the Holy Spirit had never given him any prayers for healing. It was the same for the next three nights, but he comforted her by saying that he would pray about it.

The next night as he waited before the Lord, the Spirit told him that he could take up the prayer for her, and gave him Moses' supplication in Numbers 12:13, "Heal her now, O God, I beseech thee," as well as the word he had so often been given before, in John 15:7, "If ye abide in Me . . . ye shall ask what ye will . . . ." It was a great encouragement to the woman when she knew the Lord's word had come, and there was a sensation through the village when they heard that this was to be the next challenge of faith.

Although he was ready to go deeper with God, Mr. Howells confessed that there was some fear as he entered this time of "abiding." The obedience already had been so costly that he was afraid of what might come now in gaining this new position. He was not told at the outset how long it would take, but actually he was in this prayer for six months. And, as he put it, "there was a daily obedience, a daily abiding, and a daily going through."

As the prayer continued, there were two things that were taking hold of him in ever-increasing measure. In the first place, he was arrested by that scripture, He "Himself took our infirmities, and bare our sicknesses" (Matt. 8:17), and realized for the first time that, through His atoning sarifice, the Savior had provided not only for the forgiveness of our sins but for a full redemption from all the effects of sin and the fall. Since He was "made a curse for us," why should these sufferers continue to bear the effects of that curse?

Because he believed that Christ "bare our sins in His own body on the Tree," Mr. Howells always offered to sinners not only freedom from the guilt and penalty of sin but also from the power and domination of sin. "But," he reasoned, "if He also 'bare our sicknesses,' why do I not offer healing in His Name just as freely? Why should there not be freedom from the power and dominion of sickness?" Anything less than this, he felt, was not giving to the Savior the glory He deserved, and he resolved to pay any price to prove that this power was in the atonement.

In the second place, during the "abiding" of those months he learned much more than ever before of the Holy Ghost as the Divine Intercessor. It is part of His ministry on earth to "make intercession for the saints according to the will of God . . . with groanings that cannot be uttered" (Rom. 8:26,27). The great truth that was coming to His servant with ever-increasing clearness was that the Holy Ghost can only make intercession through those human temples He indwells; also that He can never intercede in any arbitrary way, but only just as far as His channel can become one with Him in so doing.

Mr. Howells had already known something of the groanings of the Spirit in him for the needy and afflicted in the village, for Will Battery and the tramps, and the obediences that were called for. But what would it mean to intercede for someone suffering from tuberculosis? As an intercessor, he must enter into the sufferings and take the place of the one prayed for. He knew that a bedridden tubercular could have no normal home life, was confined to one room, and was cut off from everything that once comprised the interests and pleasures of life. So during this time of "abiding" the Holy Spirit went much deeper in identifying him with the suffering of others. And as He did so, it was not just this one woman but all afflicted with tuberculosis and other sufferers of the world whose burden came upon him.

Mr. Howells had not gone very far on this path before the conviction took definite hold of him that, before he was through, the Lord would literally let this disease come upon him, and that only as an actual tubercular himself would he fully be able to intercede for others suffering from this disease. That this was not a foolish imagination but a practical possibility will be seen later in his life when, after taking great personal risks to care for a tubercular, it looked as though he had contracted the disease. Moreover, in all the earlier intercessions he had literally had to take the place of, and live like, the ones prayed for.

He faced up to what this would mean, and found grace to be willing for it, if thereby the Lord could restore this mother to her family of children; and he had great joy in thinking that, after the victory in one case, the Lord might then release many more.

During the months that the Lord was speaking to him like this He was also helping the woman in a marvelous way. They were very poor, and could not afford to buy all the kinds of food she would like to have, but if there was anything she fancied, some person would be sure to walk in with that very thing. Every evening Mr. Howells and the others would come to hear her answers to prayer, and "laugh as merrily as children." All the district came to know that they were praying for her, and the doctor said she was not living on her lungs —so "she was living on prayer."

The crisis came on the evening before Good Friday. That night she told her friends that she was sinking and felt she was going to die. Mr. Howells could not take it, and urged her not to lose faith after all these months of intercession. The whole district had been told that she was going to be healed, and he could not think of taking failure now. But she persisted that she was dying.

As he left to go home, the full realization of what she had said came to him. It was a dark moment. "Dark outside," he said, "but darker inside." He sought to examine the position. Was anything wrong with his abiding? No, he had lived it "day by day, hour by hour," and the Spirit bore witness to that. "Then she is not to die," he said to the Lord. But the answer he received was unexpected. "The intercession you made was for a tubercular. Now death has come. If she is to be delivered, accept death in her place tonight."

In all sincerity he had offered himself to be a tubercular in her stead; but he had not faced the fact that the end of tuberculosis is an early death. The Lord was only asking him to do what he had said all along that he would be willing to do—to take the place of this woman that she might be delivered. But now that would mean death in a matter of hours. He had often felt there was a glow upon the Savior's words, "Greater love hath no man than this, that a man lay down his life for his friends," but now there was no glow—only darkness.

It was not that fleshly ties held him to this world, but there was the work of the mission, the souls he loved there, and the future he believed the Holy Ghost had planned for him. To leave it all then and there, and to face in cold blood that separation of soul and body, was more than he could be willing for.

He said, "It was an awful night, for I had lost the face of God. That was the first night I ever went to bed without prayer, and I made up my mind not to go any further in this life of intercession, nor to show anyone about this point of failure. All that night I blamed myself that I ever started it. It would have been better I thought, if I had gone on in a life of faith and not touched this question of healing.

"I got up the next morning not intending to go to work, but I did not go on my knees—I could not face the Holy Ghost; I felt that He was a stranger to me. I went to see my friend who was also praying for her, and the first question, as always, was, 'How is she?' Then, 'What is the last place of abiding?' I burst into tears and told him that I had failed, and could not go through. It was worse than Egyptian darkness.

"That evening the Holy Ghost spoke to me again. I shall never forget it. How sweet His voice was to me. He said, 'You didn't realize it was a privilege I offered you yesterday.' 'A privilege?' 'Yes, you were offered a place among the martyrs.' In a moment the scales fell from my eyes and I saw that glorious army of martyrs in the heavenly City, and the Savior looking for a thousand years on those who had done for Him what He did for them.

"A martyr is one who has voluntarily shortened his life down here for the Savior's sake, not merely one who dies in the course of duty; and the Lord showed me that I was to be among that number. I was afraid at first that I had forfeited my chance through my unwillingness the night before. I begged the Lord to forgive me, and I would gladly do what He asked me. I stepped into death—but there was no death there! I found that the Savior had drunk every drop of that cup for us. 'That bitter cup, love drank it up; now blessing's draught for me.' In a moment I found I was on 'the other side.' "

Caught up by the glory of what he had seen, Mr. Howells ran two miles to the sick woman's house to tell her what had happened. He called them all to pray that the Lord would make the transaction then and there—that He would heal her and take him to glory that night. He felt it could not be chance that it was Good Friday; and surely it was the Lord's will to accept his life on the day the Savior had been "obedient unto death." Many were in tears, and the woman herself refused to pray.

When he visited her the next evening, he saw at once that something had happened. Her face was radiant as an angel's and she was wanting everybody to come to her bedroom and hear about it. As she had meditated upon what Mr. Howells had told her, she was not willing for it, for he had been more than a father to her and to so many in the village; so she went on her knees in her bed and prayed, "Lord, I don't want to be healed. Don't allow any to pray for this illness to be put on him; he is more useful to You than I am, and I don't want to be delivered at his expense." The moment she prayed that, she too was caught up into His presence, and lost herself in praising her Savior. The room was filled with His glory and she went on praising all night.

"The weeks that followed were nothing less than heaven upon earth," said Mr. Howells. "We didn't pray; there was no need for prayer—we only waited for God to do His will. There was far more attraction in being called to fill the gap and go right to glory. than to be allowed to remain down here and do a little mission work. Every day for three months I expected my life to be taken, and the Lord allowed it to be like that, so that I should not be doing it under the influence of the moment. I longed to be with God. There was such reality in that song, 'The streets I am told are all paved with pure gold. And the sun it shall never go down.' "

Then, after three months, the Lord called her home suddenly. On a Saturday morning when Mr. Howells was at his work, the message came that he was wanted at once. But before he arrived, she had passed away. As he sat in the house, the Lord dealt with him for over an hour. "Although there were other people in the room," he said, "I was alone with God. He told me that although He had accepted my intercession, He was not going to take my life now; but He wanted to use me as a 'living martyr.' I had never heard such an expression before, but He made me understand that if I ever claimed any right to my life more than a dead man has, I should forfeit my position.

"So far as the case of healing was concerned, I was to walk it as a failure, and not make a word of defence. All the district knew I was praying for this woman's healing, and now I had failed openly. It was such a reaction, instead of the glory we had anticipated. Just as I came through to being willing for this, one of the converts came in. She said that before our dear sister passed away, she had left a message for me. 'Tell Rees and the others that I can't wait for them. The Savior has come for me, and I want to go with Him. Tell them I will come back to meet them' (1 Thess. 4:14). Then she had said good-bye, shaken hands all around, and had gone to be with the Lord. That glorious testimony of the first of the mission to sleep in Jesus made this 'failure' the sweetest thing in the world.

"The first test came in the funeral. Hundreds of people had gathered, because they had heard so much about her, and especially about the healing. The minister who was to officiate was not in sympathy with the work at that time. He opened his Bible at Job 13:1-5, and read, 'Lo, mine eye hath seen all this, mine ear hath heard and understood it. . . . But ye are forgers of lies, ye are all physicians of no value. Oh that ye would altogether hold your peace! and it should be your wisdom.' He was on one side of the grave and I on the other, and that in more senses than one! I heard what he said, but was unmoved as though I hadn't heard. The Lord then led me to make a few remarks on the life she lived before we went to the village, and the transformed life afterwards. The proof of it was in the triumph she had over death, for death was swallowed up in victory. I told how she had said the Lord had come to fetch her, how she wanted to go, and had said good-bye to those around her. I said, 'Have you ever heard of a person who is dying, shaking hands with everyone, as though she was going on a journey?'

"The people started to sing as in a revival. The heavens opened and the victory was such that they all started waving their handkerchiefs—even the mourners had to join in. I never pitied a man as I pitied the minister. The sad grave was turned to be the gate of heaven, and from that funeral we had the beginning of resurrection life in the mission.

"It was later that the Holy Ghost revealed why it had been necessary to take this case—'that no flesh should glory in His presence.' In a great position like this, God would not be free to use it through a person who had not first 'died' to it. It is death first and then resurrection. As the first-born and the first-fruits were to be given back to the Lord, so the first case of healing, the first-fruits of this intercession, belonged to the Lord and had to go to the altar."

12

What Is an Intercessor?

The central truth which the Holy Ghost gradually revealed to Mr. Howells and which was the mainspring of his whole life's ministry was that of intercession. The Spirit can be seen leading him into this in all His dealings with him, from the time He took full possession of him in the Llandrindod Convention until, in his dealings with the tubercular woman, the meaning of intercession became fully clear. From then onward the Spirit was constantly leading him both to gain new positions as an intercessor and to reveal the precious truths he had learned to others able to bear them. It will be useful, therefore, to stop a moment and to look a little more carefully into what is meant by being an intercessor.

That God seeks intercessors but seldom finds them is plain from the pain of His exclamation through Isaiah: "He saw that there was no man, and wondered that there was no intercessor"; and His protest of disappointment through Ezekiel: "I sought for a man among them, that should make up the hedge, and stand in the gap before Me for the land . . . but I found none."

Perhaps believers in general have regarded intercession as just some form of rather intensified prayer. It is, so long as there is great emphasis on the word "intensified"; for there are three things to be seen in an intercessor which are not necessarily found in ordinary prayer: identification, agony and authority.

The identification of the intercessor with the ones for whom he intercedes is perfectly seen in the Savior. Of Him it was said that He poured out His soul unto death; and He was numbered with the transgressors; and He bare the sin of many, and *made intercession* for the transgressors. As the Divine Intercessor, interceding for a lost world, He drained the cup of our lost condition to its last drop, He "tasted death for every man." To do that, in the fullest possible sense, He sat where we sit. By taking our nature upon Himself, by learning obedience through the things which He suffered, by being tempted in all points like as we are, by becoming poor for our sakes, and finally by being made sin for us, He gained the position in which, with the fullest authority as the Captain of our salvation made perfect through sufferings, and the fullest understanding of all we go through, He can ever live to make intercession for us, and by effective pleadings with the Father "is able to save to the uttermost them that come unto God by Him." Identification is thus the first law of the intercessor. He pleads effectively because he gives his life for those he pleads for; he is their genuine representative; he has submerged his self-interest in their needs and sufferings, and as far as possible has literally taken their place.

There is another Intercessor, and in Him we see the agony of this ministry; for He, the Holy Spirit, "maketh intercession for us with groanings which cannot be uttered." This One, the only present Intercessor on earth, has no hearts upon which He can lay His burdens, and no bodies through which He can suffer and work, except the hearts and bodies of those who are His dwelling place. Through them He does His intercessory work on earth, and they become intercessors by reason of the Intercessor within them. It is real life to which He calls them, the very kind of life, in lesser measure, which the Savior Himself lived on earth.

But before He can lead a chosen vessel into such a life of intercession, He first has to deal to the bottom with all that is natural. Love of money, personal ambition, natural affection for parents and loved ones, the appetites of the body, the love of life itself, all that makes even a converted man live unto himself, for his own comfort or advantage, for his own advancement, even for his own circle of friends, has to go to the cross. It is no theoretical death but a real crucifixion with Christ, such as only the Holy Ghost Himself can make actual in the experience of His servant. Both as a crisis and process, Paul's testimony must be made ours: "I have been and still am crucified with Christ." The self must be released from itself to become the agent of the Holy Ghost.

As crucifixion proceeds, intercession begins. By inner burdens, by calls to outward obediences, the Spirit begins to live His own life of love and sacrifice for a lost world through His cleansed channel. We see it in Rees Howells' life. We see it at its greatest height in the Scriptures. Watch Moses, the young intercessor, leaving the palace by free choice to identify himself with his slave-brethren. See him accompanying them through "the waste and howling wilderness." See him reach the very summit of intercession when the wrath of God was upon them for their idolatry and their destruction was imminent. It is not his body he now offers for them as intercessor but his immortal soul: "If Thou wilt forgive their sin—; and if not, blot me, I pray Thee, out of Thy Book"; and he actually called this "making an atonement" for them.

See the Apostle Paul, the greatest man of the new dispensation as Moses was of the old. For years his body, through the Holy Ghost, is a living sacrifice that the Gentiles might have the gospel; finally, his immortal soul is offered on the altar. The very one who was just rejoicing with the Romans that nothing could separate him and them from the love of God (Rom. 8) says a moment later, the Spirit bearing him witness, that he could wish himself "accursed [separated] from Christ for my brethren, my kinsmen according to the flesh" (Rom. 9).

This is the intercessor in action. When the Holy Ghost really lives His life in a chosen vessel there is no limit to the extremes to which He will take him in His passion to warn and save the lost. Isaiah, that aristocrat, had to go "naked and bare-footed" for three years as a warning to Israel. We can

hardly credit such a thing! Hosea had to marry a harlot, to
show his people that the heavenly Husband was willing to take
back His adulterous bride. Jeremiah was not allowed to marry,
as a warning to Israel against the terrors and tragedies of captivity. Ezekiel was not allowed to shed one tear for the death of
his wife, "the desire of his eyes." And so the list might be continued. Every greatly used instrument of God has been, in his
measure, an intercessor: Wesley for backsliding England;
Booth for the down-and-outs; Hudson Taylor for China; C.T.
Studd for the unevangelized world.

But intercession is more than the Spirit sharing His groanings with us and living His life of sacrifice for the world
through us. It is the Spirit gaining His ends of abundant grace.
If the intercessor knows identification and agony, he also
knows authority. It is the law of the corn of wheat and the
harvest: "If it die, it bringeth forth much fruit."

Intercession is not substitution for sin. There has only ever
been one substitute for a world of sinners, Jesus the Son of
God. But intercession so identifies the intercessor with the sufferer that it gives him a prevailing place with God. He moves
God. He even causes Him to change His mind. He gains his
objective, or rather the Spirit gains it through him. Thus
Moses, by intercession, became the savior of Israel and
prevented their destruction; and we can have little doubt that
Paul's supreme act of intercession for God's chosen people
resulted in the great revelation given him at that time of worldwide evangelization and the final salvation of Israel (Romans
10 and 11), and is enabling God to bring it about.

Mr. Howells would often speak of "the gained position of
intercession," and the truth of it is obvious on many occasions
in his life. It is a fact of experience. The price is paid, the obedience is fulfilled, the inner wrestlings and groanings take their
full course, and then "the word of the Lord comes." The weak
channel is clothed with authority by the Holy Ghost and can
speak the word of deliverance. "Greater works" are done. Not
only this, but a new position in grace is gained and maintained,
although even then that grace can only be appropriated and

applied in each instance under the guidance of the Spirit.

Mr. Howells used to speak of it, in Mr. Muller's phrases, as entering "the grace of faith," in contrast to receiving "the gifts of faith." What he meant was that, when we pray in a normal way, we may hope that God of His goodness will give us the thing. If He does, we rejoice; it is His gift to us; but we have no power or authority to say that we can always get that same answer at any time. Such are the gifts of faith. But when an intercessor has gained the place of intercession in a certain realm, then he has entered into "the grace of faith"; along that special line the measureless sea of God's grace is open to him. That is the gained place of intercession.

Mr. Howells referred to George Muller's experience. Mr. Muller had never gained a place of intercession over sickness, but on one occasion God raised up a sick person for whom he had prayed. On another occasion he prayed for another sick person, but there was no healing. Mr. Muller, however, said that this was not a failure in prayer because he had never gained a place of intercession over sickness, and therefore the answer to the first prayer was merely "a gift of faith," which would not necessarily be repeated. On the other hand, he had gained a place of intercession for the orphans. He was always ready to be the first sufferer on their behalf; if there was enough food for all except one, he would be the one to go without; and in this realm of supply, God held him responsible to see that the needs were always met, for the doors of God's Treasury had been permanently opened to him, and he could take as much as he needed.

Pastor Blumhardt of Germany, on the other hand, was a man who had gained a place of intercession for the sick. In his first struggles with evil spirits it took him more than eighteen months of prayer and fasting before he gained the final victory. Complaints were lodged against him of neglecting his work as a minister and devoting himself to the healing of the sick, but he said the Lord had given the parable of the friend at midnight and the three loaves and, though unworthy, he was going on knocking.

Pastor Blumhardt prayed through, and God did open. Not only were hundreds blessed, but he raised a standard for the church. After the final victory he gained such ease of access to the Throne that often, when letters came asking for prayer for sick people, after just looking up for a single moment he could find God's will as to whether they were to be healed or not. The sufferings of others became so painful to him that he was pleading for them as if for himself. That was intercession!

13

Challenging Death

Even in the face of this apparent failure with the tubercular woman, Mr. Howells knew that he had gained the position of intercession. He needed no proof himself, but was certain that the Lord would set an outward seal to the inner victory. It came a few months later.

He was called in to see a man in the village who was dying. He found him already unconscious. His wife was sobbing her heart out, for there were ten children, and he was the only bread-winner. The effect on Mr. Howells was immediate. The suffering of the woman came to him as if it were his own sister. He went out into a field and wept and, as he said, "Once you weep, or the Holy Ghost in you, you are the very one to touch the Throne."

He knew the only way to help her was to bring her husband back to her, but the man was beyond human aid. However, it seemed as if the Lord made him enter into her feelings to the point where her sufferings became his own, and her need his responsibility. God is "a Father of the fatherless," and "relieveth the widow"; so he knew that, unless he could prevail for the husband, the Holy Ghost would insist on taking that place through him, and he would be responsible to provide for this woman and support her children.

He returned to the woman's house and was sitting there, waiting for her to come downstairs, when he heard a voice speaking on a plane that seemed new to him, and saying, "He is not to die; he is to live." "The stillness that came into that room!" said Mr. Howells. "It was the stillness that God makes when He is there." The wife came down and he immediately said to her, "Since I last saw you, a great burden of prayer has been on me for your husband, and the Lord has told me he is not to die; he is to live." But she was not convinced. He could see that she hadn't taken it from him, and there was every natural reason for this: there was her husband's condition, and then the fact that the last person Mr. Howells had said would be healed had so recently died.

He left her and returned home. But as he was crossing the common the Lord began to speak to him again and said, "You didn't speak to that woman in the same way you do when you are really certain. Tomorrow morning early you must go back and tell her again, and go without doubting." It was such a strong confirmation that, as he went to bed, he declared out loud, "I'm returning tomorrow to challenge death, and say to it, 'You will not take this man!' "

As he had a train to catch the next morning at eight o'clock, he started out before six for the two-mile walk to the village. It was snowing and pitch dark, and the Evil One attacked him all the way. "It was as though legions of devils were withstanding me," he said. "I felt like a man walking against the tide, and the enemy kept saying, 'The man died as soon as you left last night.' " It was a severe test of faith, but after battling his way through, as he got near the house "it was sweet to see the light."

When he entered, he said to the woman, "I don't blame you for not taking what I told you yesterday. I didn't say it to you with the certainty with which I tell things that I know, but I have come over this morning to tell you now that your husband will not die; and as a proof of what I say, if he should die, I will support you and your children." She brightened visibly, as she really took it from him this time, and he returned in great joy, very differently from the way he had come. "It seemed as though heaven had come down to rejoice, and I

knew death could never take him. There was no death there,''
he said.

He was away for two days, during which he refused to take
note of the enemy's attacks. As he was returning, the devil still
kept at it, telling him they would be waiting to give him the
news that the man had died, and to ask him to speak at the
funeral! When he arrived at the station, some of the believers
were waiting for him and one called out, "He is out of danger.
The moment you left the house he changed for the better!"

The next case was harder. It was a woman who was one of
their best converts, in whose home they held cottage meetings.
She was the wife of one William Davies, and sister-in-law to
the tubercular woman. She was dangerously ill after the birth
of a child, and the doctor had given no hope of her recovery.

When Mr. Howells went to the home, they were all crying.
"Do you know the Lord's will?" was William Davies' first
eager question. "He hasn't revealed it yet," Rees answered,
"but I don't believe He would take her without telling me."
That was the first ray of light. There was no time for delay,
and William in his anxiety pressed him further. "Do you think
He will speak today?" "I believe He will," Rees reassured him.
"I'll walk home now, and I am sure He will speak to me."

The vital question, of course, was: What was God's will?
Even though an intercession had been gained, the Lord's will
must be revealed in each case; and in this one the very fact that
he wanted her to live could sway his judgment. Only the impartial can find God's will, as the Savior said in John 5:30. On
that two-mile walk God always talked with His servant. "I
have called you friends" was no idle theory to him, but a
precious and practical relationship. He always expected the
Master to share these secrets with him. So as they walked that
day, the Lord's word came to him again, "She will be healed
and not die." "The moment I heard it," Rees said, "I had the
joy of healing."

He returned in the early afternoon, because every minute
counted. He could even joke with William Davies a bit now.
"If I tell you God's will, will you believe me? If you do, and I

tell you your wife is to get well, mind there are no more tears! If you want to cry, you had better cry now before I tell you!" "The Holy Ghost was in the house," Mr. Howells said, "and I knew He had conquered death. Naturally speaking, death was in the room, but I was in perfect peace. We got down and prayed, about six of the children joining us. What a praise meeting we had, and she changed for the better that day!"

Through the position gained in his intercession for the tubercular woman God's servant had become sensitive to His voice in cases of sickness in a way that he had never been before. It had been a long spiritual climb in her case, but now he found that in a moment he could take the word of the Lord. He had so many of these cases at that time that it looked as if this would be his special ministry; and he often said from that period that he believed a new era of healing would break forth in the Christian church. Perhaps only eternity will reveal how much the Spirit's intercession and believing through him has contributed to the revival of spiritual healing which has been witnessed in many parts of the church in recent years.

14

A Father to Orphans

When the tubercular woman died, she left four little children. It was such a test for her husband that he fell into bad habits through drink, and much neglected them. Mr. Howells one day was burdened about this. The Lord showed him plainly that something would have to be done for these children. The Lord asked Rees what He should do with them, but Mr. Howells gave Him no reply. The Spirit said, "Unless you give Me an answer, they will have to go to the workhouse." Then He asked him, "If anything happened to your brother or sister-in-law, would you allow their children to go there?" "Certainly I wouldn't," answered Mr. Howells. "Why do you answer Me so quickly about your own fold," the Lord said, "yet you have nothing to say about these four little orphans?" "Well, of course, blood is thicker than water." "Yes, but *spirit* is thicker than blood!"

Things came to a crisis when the father went away and left the children. Mr. Howells' first thought was that he would make himself responsible for them, as a guardian, and pay a woman to go to the house to look after them. That was more than many would have done, but the Lord said to him, "It is a father they need—not a guardian. I am a Father of the fatherless, but I cannot be a Father to them in heaven, so I must be one through you."

He had to face up to what that would mean—to make a home with them and earn enough to keep them until the youngest was of age. It would mean fifteen to twenty years of his life going, and all the hopes he had of one day taking the message of the Holy Ghost to the world. Moreover, they were not his children; he did not have a father's love for them, and there was nothing in him that wanted to do it.

It was the first test on the reality of his position as a martyr, and it came suddenly against him. It was on this that the Spirit challenged him. He was to have taken the mother's place in tuberculosis and death. But the Lord had taken her and brought him back as a "living martyr." If that was real, then he must take her place now in caring for her four little ones. There was no answer to that, and he dare not question the authority of the Holy Ghost in his life.

"But," he said, "you must have God's nature to love other people's children as your own." So he told the Lord, "I am willing for You to be a Father through me, but I cannot do it unless *You* love them through me, so that they are not like adopted but begotten children. And to do that, You will have to change my nature."

Really, Rees never thought God could do it, but He did! One night by his bedside he found God's love pouring into him—His love for the fatherless. There were no bounds to it. It went out towards those four little children—nothing now could stop him going to live with them. He felt that they had a claim on him. He put it this way, "Any child without parents has a claim on God to be a Father to him, so these four orphans had a claim on the Holy Spirit who was to be a Father to them through me." But divine love could not be limited to four. He said, "I felt I loved every little child in the world that had no one to look after it. It was the love of God flowing through me."

He arranged for someone to look after the children temporarily while he made all preparations to go and live with them. It was no test to him now, but all joy! However, on the very day that he was to go, three sisters of their mother said they would like to take them and give them a home. The Lord showed him that this was His provision for them, but that he had gained the position of "a father to the orphans."

The proof of the reality of this was to be seen in the coming years. No one could live with Mr. Howells in his later days in the Bible College and see him and Mrs. Howells taking and loving children of missionaries and Jewish refugee children, some in their own home, and many in the happy home for misssionaries' children near by, without realizing the extent to which God had indeed given them the father and mother heart, which could gather, not four, but seventy, under their wings.

Commenting later on this, Mr. Howells said: "The place of intercession gained at that time holds good today. There was no need for the Lord to test it over again, unless there had been indifference or backsliding. From that gained position one can continually pray for the orphans and ask the Lord to be a Father to them, even through others, because one only asks Him to do through another what he is willing for the Lord to do through him. This is the law of intercession on every level of life: that only so far as we have been tested and proved willing to do a thing ourselves can we intercede for others. Christ is our Intercessor because He took the place of each one prayed for.

"We are never called to intercede for sin; that has been done once and for all. But we are often called to intercede for sinners and their needs, and the Holy Ghost can never 'bind the strong man' through us on a higher level than that in which He has first had victory in us.'"

In a wonderful way the Lord also used Mr. Howells to reveal His love to the father who had deserted the children. For over sixteen years, since he had been a boy, Mr. Howells had paid money into the Rechabites Sick Benefit Club, a cooperative form of insurance plan for the village. Now the Lord told him that he was not to keep his payment up any longer. "As the Lord had the ownership of the money," said Mr. Howells, "I could not use it without His permission. The devil was busy warning me that I would have no provision for a rainy day and, in plain language, my end would be in the workhouse —and all my life I had dreaded even the name of that place!" But the Lord made him stand on one scripture: "He that gathered much had nothing over; and he that had gathered little had no lack" (2 Cor. 8:15). So the Rechabite Club had "to go to the altar," nor was he allowed to put in a claim for the amounts already paid.

But three months after the man had deserted his children and had also been compelled to leave the district through a sin he had committed, Mr. Howells was guided, strangely enough, to pay the arrears on the man's Sick Benefit Club, and thereafter to keep it up to date. It was a surprising guidance, for if it had been wrong for him to pay his own Club money, how could it be right to pay this man's?

The Holy Ghost revealed that the wrong for him had not been in paying the Club but in the motive he had in maintaining his payments. God had called him to the school of faith and therefore, for him, the position of faith once gained would be a complete substitute for the Club against the workhouse. "But it was equally clear," said Mr. Howells, "that we cannot say a thing is wrong for others just because we have been called to give it up; it depends on our position or grade in life." So he paid this man's Club, and no one else knew about it.

He never heard a word from the man till about five months later when he had a letter from him saying that he was laid up in bed with tuberculosis and had had a severe hemorrhage. For two weeks he had struggled with himself to go on his knees and ask the Lord for forgiveness, but he had been too much ashamed to do so because he had dishonored "the blessed Name." But one Sunday morning the Salvation Army workers had come in front of the house where he was staying, and while they were singing he had gotten out of bed, went on his knees, and received forgiveness and peace. He was now writing to say how sorry he was that he had yielded to temptation and disgraced the mission through the sin into which he had fallen, and asked the friends to forgive him, since the Lord had done so. He had no money to pay his lodgings, but the doctor had arranged for him to be taken to the workhouse the following week.

When the man heard what Mr. Howells had done for him,

the love of God broke him down. Instead of the workhouse, he was taken to his father's home and had a guinea a week for five months, until he passed peacefully away into the presence of the Lord. The little ones received £38 after his death. The incident had a great effect on the village and was also a proof to His servant that the Lord could not only keep him out of the workhouse but also keep others through him if he gave perfect obedience to the Holy Spirit.

In all these experiences the Lord had a twofold purpose: the blessing of the needy and the transformation of His servant. "The Holy Ghost took me through grade after grade," he said. "The process of changing one's natures (replacing the self nature by the divine nature) was very slow and bitter. It was a daily dying and showing forth the life of Christ, but that life was the life of a victim. Christ was the greatest Victim on one side of the cross but the greatest Victor on the other. The daily path was the way of the cross: every selfish motive and every selfish thought was at once dealt with by the Holy Spirit. In my boyhood days the strictest man I knew was my schoolmaster, but how often I said that the Holy Ghost was a thousand times more strict—the schoolmaster could only judge by actions, but the Holy Ghost was judging by the motive."

One evening, for instance, Rees and his friend were to both speak in the open air. The friend preached first, and the Holy Ghost so used him that Mr. Howells began to wonder how he could ever preach after him (Mr. Howells not being a gifted open-air speaker). This grew into a thought of jealousy.

"No one knew it," he said, "but that night the Holy Ghost whipped me and humbled me to the dust. He showed me the ugliness of it and how the devil would take advantage of such a thing to damage the souls of those people. I never saw a thing I hated more than that, and I could have cursed myself for it. 'Didn't you come out to the open air for these souls to be blessed?' He asked. 'And if so, what difference does it make through whom I bless them?' He told me to confess the sin to my friend, and if ever He found it in me again, I would have to make a public confession.

"From that day on I have not dared to cherish a thought of jealousy, because not once did the Holy Ghost go back on His word to me. Whatever warning of punishment He had given me, if I disobeyed, I had to pay the full penalty. A person might think it was a life of bondage and fear. It would be to the flesh, but to the new man in Christ it was a life of fullest liberty.

"At first I had a tendency to pity myself and grumble at the penalty for disobedience, but as I saw that I must either lose this corrupt self here or bear the shame of its exposure hereafter, I began to side with the Holy Spirit against myself, and looked on the stripping as a deliverance rather than a loss."

15

Lord Radstock

At the Llandrindod Convention in August 1909 Mr. Howells again met his friend Mr. John Gosset, with whom he had had the correspondence about the New Year card. Hearing Rees speak in one of the meetings on prayer and intercession, Mr. Gosset was so blessed that he told his friend, Lord Radstock, about it. As a result, Mr. Howells was asked by him to address a special meeting of believers. He told them what he had proved in his experience of the difference between a prayer warrior and an intercessor, and the points he stressed are worth recording, though touched on in a previous chapter.

A prayer warrior can pray for a thing to be done without necessarily being willing for the answer to come through himself; and he is not even bound to continue in the prayer until it is answered. But an intercessor is responsible to gain his objective, and he can never be free till he has gained it. He will go to any lengths for the prayer to be answered through himself. But once a position of intercession has been gained, tested and proved, the intercessor can claim all the blessings on that grade, whenever it is God's will for him to do so. It is the same as in Euclid, Mr. Howells pointed out: up to the grade a person has learned the propositions he can do the riders on them, but not any farther, and there is never need to go over the same ground twice, unless he is uncertain of them.

During his address Mr. Howells also touched on divine healing, and told of the Lord's dealings with him over the tubercular woman: how the first gained case had to go to the altar, because the first-fruits belong to God; and how, although the Holy Spirit witnessed in him that he had gained it, he had to walk it as a failure; and how through that the Lord gave such a sentence of death to the flesh that in all future cases of healing self would take no glory.

In telling this, Rees had no idea that Lord Radstock had been led the same way. The story was afterwards recorded in his biography. He had accepted the truth of divine healing, through James 5:15, "The prayer of faith shall save the sick, and the Lord shall raise him up," and pledged himself to act on it. Indeed, he believed the Church's neglect of this command was the cause of much suffering.

After he had taken this stand, his eldest daughter fell seriously ill. He had many doctors among his religious friends but felt led to refuse their help, yet in spite of his faith in God's word, "heaven was silent and the child died." Standing over her death-bed Lord Radstock was enabled to say, "Though He slay me, yet will I trust Him." It was a tremendous test of his faith and caused him great personal agony, but out of the affliction he came forth more than a conqueror and was afterwards used in hundreds of cases of divine healing. However, Lord Radstock had never understood why his daughter had died until he heard Mr. Howells. He took immediate hold on the word about the first-fruits going to the altar, but it did make him wonder how the Lord had been able to reveal these laws to His young servant.

This explanation made such an impression on Lord Radstock that he told Rees Howells God had given him light which should be passed on to the church of Christ and, as a university training would be an advantage, he would like him to go to College at his expense. Lord Radstock also took Rees to see many of his friends and asked him to repeat this same point to them. But as Mr. Howells said, concerning God's claim on the first-fruits: "Only a person near it would see it."

Mr. Gosset was so pleased with the result of the visit that he told Rees he would like him to meet many of his friends in

London, including Sir Robert Anderson, the Postmaster General, and so he invited him to come up as his guest. This was the opening of a new door—for the young miner to meet "people of rank"! As he said, "Nothing pleased the natural man better than that, and my first thought was, 'You don't know where all this will end!' New openings were coming from many directions, but this one pleased me more than any, and I had some secret satisfaction in making it known to my friends. When I told them at home, they too were very pleased and thought it would be the finish of this strange life, the plain food and so on! Outwardly it was a great honor to be asked to speak on prayer and intercession to such men as Lord Radstock and Sir Robert Anderson, but I little thought what a great lesson the Lord had to teach me through it."

16

Called to a Hidden Life

About a month after receiving the invitation from Mr. Gosset there came a new call to intercession. Although many drunkards in the village had been gloriously converted, there were some men that they failed to get through. They attended the meetings and showed a desire to follow the Lord but were such terrible slaves to drink that the enemy still kept his hold on them. There was a need once again to "bind the strong man and spoil his goods." Actually, the intercession proved to be the first step away from a public ministry into a hidden life.

For three years, after his day's work was done, Rees Howells had been at the mission every night. There were meetings five evenings a week and the other two were spent in visiting. His work in the pit took him from 7 a.m. to 4:30 p.m., and then he had the two-mile walk each way in all weathers. There was no time to attend any other meetings, for he hardly ever left his flock, except during the week of the Llandrindod Convention to which they took as many of the new converts as possible. The work had become so well established that many people were coming in from the surrounding districts on Sunday evenings; it was like a continuous revival.

The outward effect on the village had been that, whereas three years before, the brewery was sending up two wagons and a cart loaded with barrels of beer every fortnight on pay days, it had now come down to one cart, and that only half full. It was a common joke that it would have paid the brewery to have persuaded Rees Howells and his friends to become shareholders!

"The only enemy we had," said Mr. Howells, "was the devil himself! All the people respected us, for they knew we were out for their welfare. Although inwardly we were often going through trials and testings, they were never told of these; it was a perpetual revival with them. Oh, how precious the Name of Jesus was to us! In the open-air meetings, the district rang with 'Blessed Be the Name of the Lord!' "

The difficulty Mr. Howells had was to find time for prayer. Really his only opportunity was on that two-mile walk to the mission, one mile of which was over a lonely common. He always tried to be alone for that mile and, after leaving the last house behind, would remove his cap and continue in the attitude of prayer. The conventions of those days made it an unheard-of thing *not* to wear a head covering when out of doors. But when alone, the presence of God was so real that he always bared his head.

This became so much a habit that he never once crossed the common without putting his cap in his pocket, and when returning late at night, after the lights in the town were put out, he would go the whole way like that. But curious though it may seem to us today, *nothing* would have induced him to go hatless in the daytime! As he said, "The hatless brigade was unknown at that time!"

This apparently trivial habit was the first thing used by the Spirit to make him dead to the influence of the public. One Sunday morning very early, he was with the Lord in prayer. "The glory of that morning was far brighter than the light of the sun. There was such a peace and solemn hush that I felt the place was holy ground. I had felt it sometimes before, but it was far more intense that morning, as though Isaiah's words had become a fact: 'And the light of the sun shall be sevenfold, as the light of seven days.' The Lord then showed me that the place of abiding in the intercession to which He had called me, was to keep in the attitude of prayer all day. For the first time I could not take my hat with me! To walk through the town, to go to the mission would be impossible! I could never do it! *Never!*

"The glory soon passed away, and the sun had no more light than usual—if anything, less—and oh, the darkness that came over me! How I wished I had not gone out that morning. Even fasting was not to be compared with this humiliation. Only those at home were involved in the test of fasting, but in this thing I was to be a spectacle before the whole town. Never had they seen a man out of doors without a hat!"

When the time for the mission came, the Holy Ghost told him he was not to go unless he obeyed. While he was on his knees, the Lord asked him his reasons for not wanting to obey. Did he want to go out of the Lord's presence? No, it wasn't that. The only reason he could give was that the influence of the public would be too great over him, and he wouldn't be able to stand it. The Lord told him that was the very reason why He had asked him to do it, and he was not to preach again on being dead to the world until he had victory over it.

"How much of the world is in us, when we often think we are dead to it!" commented Mr. Howells. "I used to laugh about a man who had put the Salvation Army cap on, but I wished that day that the Holy Ghost would allow me to wear even that! But He would allow no compromise. I had to say, 'I am a bondslave; You pull me through.' "

The Howells family was well known and highly respected in the town, and the thought of disgracing his parents made the test doubly hard. Rees thought if he could avoid his mother he would not mind so much, because this, on top of the fasting, would be sure to make her think that something was wrong with him. He would go to any lengths to avoid hurting her feelings. "I was upstairs praying," he remembered, "trying to get as much strength as possible, but the Lord seemed to be very far away. Often in a test it seems that there is no God in the world."

His mother knew he was later than usual and heard him coming downstairs. She came to meet him with his hat in her hand, brushing it for him with a mother's loving care. "When I told her I was not wearing a hat," he recalled, "I thought of old Simeon's words to Mary: 'A sword shall pierce through thine own soul also.' What it means for parents to see one of their sons walking on a strange path!

"I shall never forget going through the town that day and passing people going to other churches. Talk about being dead to the world! Every sensitive nerve in me was alive to the world's influence! I was not much better than a blind man. It seemed that the devil had gathered all the forces of hell to attack this simple obedience. In itself, there was nothing to it; I was only called to spend the day in the attitude of prayer and that meant a little separation from the world.

"Oh, the depths of this respectable self-nature—but it was in the process of being changed for the divine nature! It was a deliverance to reach the mission. It was like the City of Refuge from the avenger of blood, and among ourselves there was always a laugh after a test."

But it was not only on Sundays the attitude of prayer was to be maintained. "Whether working, walking or anything else," the souls for whom he was praying were to be upon his heart; so that meant going every day without his hat. "To an extent I had victory over that," he said, "but it was a real death to go to work without it. However, it had now become harder to disobey than to obey, and the people became used to it."

In separating him to Himself, the Lord was preparing to take Rees much farther than this. He was going to call him away from public ministry altogether and the next step came through an attack of the enemy on his special friend and co-worker in the mission. They loved each other and "by nature," observed Mr. Howells, "he was one of the most lovable persons I had ever met. Also, like Apollos, he was eloquent and mighty in the Scriptures." But the enemy, through some believers, began to tell his friend that so long as he remained with Rees Howells in the village he would never be at his best. He needed to have a work of his own.

The Lord showed Mr. Howells the seriousness of this attack, and that he was the only one who could save his friend: "The only way you can do it is by giving him the very thing the enemy says he will never get. Why don't you give the leadership of the mission to him? Retire behind and be an intercessor for him. Pray that the mission will be a greater success in his hands than in yours." And He reminded Rees that this was one of the very things He had spoken to him about years before at Llandrindod.

He had to face the effect it would have on his life. "For three years I had put all my time, money and everything into the mission," he noted, "and had been over every night. And now, when there were great prospects, He was asking me to step down and help behind my friend, as he had previously helped behind me. The mission was growing, and would become still more popular, and the people naturally would attribute all the success to my friend. They would never see nor remember that it needed someone to put down the foundation.

"It was a great inward conflict to allow my friend to get the outward success. This was the next grade of self the Holy Ghost was going to deal with; and it was a hard process, allowing self to be replaced by His divine nature. For three days I could not willingly accept it, but I knew I would be pulled through. It was God's way of working one up to having as much joy in a hidden life as in an open and successful one. If my aim in life was to do God's will, then I could truly say either way would be equal joy."

The story of Madame Guyon, in which the process of sanctification was to be seen very plainly, proved a help to him at this time. Even in the dungeon in France she would say, "I ask no more, in good or ill, but union with Thy holy will."

God brought Rees through and made another deep change in his nature. Like Jonathan, he was able to love the man who took his place. He talked it over with his friend and told him how God was leading him and that from henceforth the mission would be his while he stood behind him in prayer. "Build it as a great mission. The Lord will win souls through you, and

I will be praying for you. I want the mission to become a greater success through you than it was through me."

17

The Hatless Brigade

Shortly after Mr. Howells had handed over the mission to his friend, the anticipated letter came from London asking him to go up the following week to be Mr. Gosset's guest. His first thought was that he couldn't go, because he had been called to gain this new place of intercession and it would take three months. He went to bed feeling he had made a real sacrifice, but the next morning the Lord asked him, "Why are you not going to London?" "Because of my intercession." "Why, can't you intercede in London?"

The Holy Spirit would always probe down to the very root of the self He wanted to get at. "Tell Me your real reason for not going," He insisted. Mr. Howells had to confess that it was because he could not face going to London without his hat! "I had victory over being without one at home," he said, "but going to London like that to be the guest of people of rank was out of the question. I knew Mr. Gosset would never allow me to insult him. I was sensitive to other people's feelings and, after his kindness, I would have refused any amount of money rather than do that.

"The hundred and one excuses the flesh made! But the Holy Ghost would have none of them. He had planned all this to prove whether I would obey Him rather than man. People say very flippantly sometimes that it is an honor to be a fool for Christ's sake—but it is quite another thing actually to be called to do it by the Holy Ghost!"

The conflict was sharp. It even came into his mind momentarily whether it was possible to turn back from "this life of surrender, this bondslave life, this daily dying, and just live an ordinary Christian life, and preach the gospel and help the poor," as many of his friends did. But the Spirit held him to the reality of his "living martyr" position, with no more claim on his life down here than a dead man has. There was some questioning, as there always was until he actually came up to becoming one with the Holy Ghost in what He was doing, but he knew he had no choice in the matter, and he would not dare show any real unwillingness lest he should forfeit the privilege of his martyr position.

The Spirit "who never pushes" drew him with the cords of love by showing him the bitter cross the Lord bore. As the Scripture says: "He had no form nor comeliness; He was despised and rejected of men, smitten of God and afflicted."

"In the mission," observed Mr. Howells, "we used to sing:

Where He leads me I will follow . . .
I'll go with Him through the Garden,
I'll go with Him all the way.

But what a struggle it was to go with Him now! I asked Him to show me through the Scriptures that He had called His servants to do this kind of thing before, in case Mr. Gosset and his friends asked me to give them Scripture for what I was doing. If He did that, then I said I would go.

"Like a flash He brought before me John the Baptist and Elijah: the one clothed only in a garment of camel's hair and his food locusts and wild honey; the other spending three and a half years between a cave and a widow's home, where they were eating the last meal every day. This had been their way of the cross to power.

"The Lord would always corner me, and then I would laugh and say, 'Yes, Lord; You pull me through!' So I gave in, but this time I had grumbled a little, and when He reminded me of John the Baptist I was afraid He might send me to London lacking more than just a hat! So I kept myself busy all that day, in case He would add a little more to the obedience."

The day came to go to London. His mother had become used to his being without a hat in his own home town, but she had it ready and well brushed that morning. That was the first test! The devil also suggested to him that it would be better to take a cap in his pocket in case it rained; but he had to say that an umbrella would be more appropriate!

When the train was steaming into Paddington, he said he felt like a man going to the scaffold! Mr. Gosset was there to meet him and gave him a royal welcome as he stepped out of the carriage. Then he put his head into the compartment and said, "You have left your hat behind." "No, I didn't bring one with me." "What! Coming to London without a hat! Oh dear no! You must realize, Rees, that you are not in the country now. You cannot come to London without a hat." "Then I must go back." "It is not a question of going back," Mr. Gosset replied, "it is a question of wearing a hat."

"I never pitied any man as I did my host," said Mr. Howells, "when we drove from Paddington to Piccadilly in an open cab. He was as red as a lobster. On the way he said, 'I have a new cap at home, and it is a very expensive one. It does not fit me, and I will give it you.' I had to tell him then that if I were given all the caps in London for wearing one that side of Christmas, I would not take them, because to go without a hat was one of my positions of abiding to gain a place of intercession.

"He told me afterwards that his pride had never been touched as it was then. The Lord had tried to reach it before, but he would not allow anyone to get near it. He said he had blushed more during that drive than in all his lifetime before."

If the cap had aroused such conflict, what about the fasting and plain food? What would he think of "Daniel's menu"? While waiting for the meal, he read out to Mr. Howells all the invitations to dinner. "What a burden came over me!" Rees said. "Another stand had to be made. I knew I could only take two meals a day of the simplest food, so what was the use of the dinners?

"I didn't say a word; I could never speak until I was compelled to, and I didn't have too much strength to tell it even then! The bell went and we sat down to dinner. 'All this has been prepared for you,' he said, 'and I want you to taste everything on the table.' Then I had to confess that for the next three months I was only to take two meals a day, of bread and cheese and soup!

"He put both hands up and exclaimed, 'What have you done with me, Rees? Who will they say my guest is? One of the old prophets?' We both had a great laugh and I told him the test it had been to me to obey the Lord and go to London. I told him that to insult him after all his kindness was more than I had bargained for when I took my place of abiding. 'To think you are doing all this to reach lost souls,' was his reply, 'and here I am now an old man, and I have done practically nothing to reach them.' Then he told me, 'Don't disobey God even if the king should invite you to dinner!' At the same time he said, 'I can't walk with you in Piccadilly! You will have to walk two yards in front or two yards behind me!' We laughed for hours. Such a cross, but such a glorious victory!"

Mr. Gosset took him to visit his friends, and he had "a great welcome and a great time with them all, especially with Lord Radstock and Sir Robert Anderson. The Lord was testing me to see whether that class of society would touch me, and I could say I was dead to it all."

But only on the last day did God's real purpose in the visit come to light. The night before he left, Mr. Gosset came to his room and said, "God has revealed something to me. He has told me He is going to bless my house because you are here, as He blessed the house of Obed-edom because the Ark of God was there." As he spoke, Mr. Howells said, "The place was filled with God; I could hardly stand it."

The next morning the Lord led Mr. Howells to read about the Shunammite woman and to say to Mr. Gosset, "Do you know you have done exactly the same to me as that woman did to the prophet? And I too am to ask, 'What is to be done for thee?' Any blessing you would like from God He is going to give you."

The host broke down and wept. He had one great desire, he said: that his son in the army, Captain Ralph Gosset, who had left the paths in which he was brought up, and was now returning from Africa, should not bring discredit on the family. "God will do more than that," answered Mr. Howells. "He will not return to the army without being a converted man." It was to be a fulfillment of the Savior's word to the seventy: "Whatsoever house ye enter, first say, 'Peace be to this house.' And if the son of peace be there, your peace shall rest upon it."

29ᵗʰ Oct. 1909.

89, PICCADILLY. W.

It is the desire of my heart that
Ralph should be converted.
and Rees Howells is in full
Sympathy and has agreed to
take the place of intercession
for this great mercy. it is our
desire that he will be converted
before his return from leave.—
          Rees Howells   A. Gosset

18

The Vow of a Nazarite

The path of intercession that Mr. Howells was following now took on a new definiteness and began to go steeply upwards. The hard cases on whose account he had been called back for further intercession had all been in the village and under his personal influence. But in Mr. Gosset's son there was a soul whom he had never seen and probably would never meet, whom he had no possible means of influencing except by way of the Throne. The Lord said to him, "This will be the test case of your intercession."

It was evident that the Lord had been preparing His servant to gain a much higher position than he had realized, and for this he was going to be turned aside from his work among men to deal only with God. The prayer was made quite definite by being written on a card, signed by both Mr. Gosset and himself, of which they each kept a copy. Mr. Howells counted it as one of the most precious things in his possession.

On returning from London, as part of his abiding, Rees was called to be on his knees for three hours every evening, from 6 to 9 p.m., after he had returned from the mine. He saw how the Lord was preparing him for this when a few weeks before He had him give up the leadership of the mission to his friend. Now he was called to give up all spiritual activities outside, and he was not even to attend meetings in the mission. He was to read the Bible through on his knees, which indeed was the way he always read it, and the Holy Ghost would be his Teacher.

"It took a little time before I could learn to be absolutely quiet in His presence," he recalled. "I had been so used to preaching that, whenever I had new light on the Word, I was apt to preach without knowing it, although there were no people there! I had to pull myself up all the time." The initial conditions of the abiding were: (1) Fasting—two meals a day. (2) Living in the attitude of prayer—which meant being hatless. (3) Giving up all outward work at the mission, and not going to one service. (4) The three hours each evening to be spent on his knees—two hours in reading the Word, and the last one in waiting before God. Rees knew there were to be other places of abiding, but they were not yet given.

This life was different indeed from the one he had been living—to be hidden away after years of activity. Instead of fellowship with Christians, it was to be only with the Lord. He was not even allowed to make known at home, nor to the wider circle of his friends, that he had given up the mission to his friend and by choice had entered this path of intercession. So a rumor went about that something in the visit to London had been a disappointment and had caused him to give up the mission and never attend a place of worship!

At first Rees felt he could never draw such joy from this hidden life as he had in active work. It seemed a great tragedy to him that he was getting much light on the Word and there was no outlet for it. He even had the idea that God would never allow him to preach again.

Another disadvantage was that it was not so easy to pray in the evenings as in the mornings because the happenings of the day made an impression on his mind and, at first, it was difficult to shake them off. "Although we may be away from the presence of people, how hard it is," he used to say, "to silence the voices of self. But after a time the Lord brought me to the place where the moment I shut the door at six o'clock, I left the world outside and had access into the presence of God. It was perfect fellowship. I could truly say, 'So nigh, so very nigh to God, I cannot nearer be; For in the person of His Son, I am as near as He.' ''

The Lord then told him that he must be open to be taken by Him into any position that the prophets or apostles took. "I saw how the iniquity of the nation was laid upon Ezekiel," he said, "but I wasn't afraid of being tested in food like him. Neither was I afraid of Jeremiah, but I *was* afraid of Isaiah! There was never a prophet like that man—of royal blood and one of the greatest statesmen and writers. But I saw how the Holy Ghost humiliated him in what He called him to do (Isaiah 20). The only comfort I had was that by starting to read at Genesis, it would take me about two months before I reached him! But much sooner than that I reached something else and I couldn't escape it.

"I wasn't tested in Genesis, but I came to Numbers 6:2-6, 'When either man or woman separate themselves to vow the vow of a Nazarite . . . all the days of the vow of his separation, there shall no razor come upon his head . . . he shall be holy and shall let the locks of the hair of his head grow . . . he shall come at no dead body.' And the Holy Ghost said to me, 'For the period of this intercession you are to live like this. If your father or mother die, you are not to go near them, and on no account are you to use a razor.'

"I told the Lord it would be far better to die than to do this. I was just thirty years old and one of six brothers who had all lived a most respectable life. I knew they would never allow a thing like that at home. To go without a hat was bad enough, but this was a thousand times worse! I thought that every man who grew a beard at least trimmed it every week, but a Nazarite could not touch his hair or beard. And the devil whispered, 'At this rate, in six months it will be down to your knees, and the only place fit for you will be the asylum! It would not be so bad if you only went there yourself, but the worst of it is, you will send your parents there also.'

"I told the Holy Spirit I knew of no one who had been called to such a thing in this generation—how could I ever give in to it? But, as always, He insisted in getting at the real reason for unwillingness. Excuses would never do for Him. 'Tell Me the truth,' He insisted. 'Why are you not willing to walk like Samuel and John the Baptist?' 'Because of my parents,' I answered. 'Do You mean me to put them in the grave or in an asylum?' And I really thought this was the reason.

"But the Lord said, 'Put your parents on the cross. My mother was in the crowd when I hung on the cross—the greatest Victim the world has ever known. You tell me the *real* reason why you are not willing to do it.'

"So I told Him, 'The real reason is that the influence of people will be too strong for me, and I am afraid of being overcome by it.' 'Exactly!' He returned. 'And that is the reason why I want you to do it. If there is no world in you, how can the world influence you? Has it ever influenced a dead person? You will be a Nazarite until all that is taken out of you.' He also added, 'Is not a beard anyhow more natural for a man than shaving?' And I had to admit it was.

"I said one more thing to the Lord: 'It was bad enough for me to take tramps home—but for me to *be* a tramp! I know my brothers will never live with me. Let me go to lodgings.' But He answered, 'No, you must walk it at home. Before you gain this position every natural affection, every tender tie must be broken until the souls of other people become to you the same as the souls of your own.' " He knew he had to go through with it; it was no use kicking against the pricks. As usual, Rees had to say, "Pull me through!" and, indeed, he needed pulling.

There were a few days' grace before the people at home or the outside world would notice the absence of the razor; Rees had to be prepared for the effect upon them. This was all taking place just a few weeks after there seemed such prospects for his life through the invitation to London. Mr. Gosset's father was a personal friend of King Edward VII, and Rees' visit to Mr. Gosset's home was an event in his own father's life. There had even been a notice of it in the local paper and he knew that it came from his father.

It was altogether right for people to see that a person with the Holy Ghost can keep company with lords as well as with tramps! His parents were really proud of him and looked forward to another opening. In all the strange paths through which he had been led in the previous few months they had never doubted his sincerity; their only objection was that he allowed things to go too far. But now there was to be *this* crowning folly!

The first thing they noticed was that he did not go out on week nights as usual, so they wondered what was wrong in the mission. Then they saw that he did not come downstairs on Sunday. His father and mother themselves stayed back from chapel that day, and he could hear them whispering downstairs. "What has happened to him? Was he disappointed in his visit to London?" Finally, when they noticed that he had not shaved and was spending all his time in his room, they knew the worst had come!

"I drank that cup to the bottom," Mr. Howells said. "It cost me to do this to my parents, and they would have done anything to prevent my being an open failure in the eyes of the public. How I wished I could give a word of explanation! That would have made up for everything; but no, the path was, 'He opened not His mouth.' That was as painful to me as the actual death I was to go through before the outside world.

"It was a great death. It was the talk between every two. The flesh was not to be spared on any point. Many thought my outward appearance was the result of failure, but they could not detect where the failure had come. Even my clothes at that time were enough to make my people ashamed of me, because the Lord had made me give away my best and keep only one suit.

"For the first two weeks I did not have victory, and going to work was a most painful experience. During the time I had walked about with Will Battery (those years before when the people had turned around and stared) I used to blush, for I had never seen a man like him—never shaved, hair long, shoes unlaced. I had thought then, 'I am blushing to walk with him; but supposing I took his place!' It came on me at that time that the Savior took his place, died his death, and brought all that disgrace on His own earthly family, while I was sensitive and blushed just to be with him. It came to me then, too, 'One day you will have to walk like that'; and as sure as He said it, I was now having to do it. If I blushed at all when I passed certain people, He made me walk that same way again. He watched me on every point until I became as dead as a person who has really died. It was only the value of a lost soul that made me do it."

The criticism Rees received was not only from the world— much of it was from the religious people. They said they knew he was going too far; they had prophesied this fall and now it had come. It was the experience of Psalm 69:8, "I am become a stranger unto my brethren, and an alien unto my mother's children." And the reason is given in the following verse: "For the zeal of thine house hath eaten me up; and the reproaches of them that reproached thee are fallen upon me." Only a very few of the inner circle knew that it was by choice he had taken this way of intercession, and that the Holy Spirit was making him tread himself that very path of shame into which so many drift because of sin. The world thought he was "like the monks, or had taken a silly notion into his head," or that it was the effect of failure and that he had gone out of his mind.

We can only imagine what this meant to Miss Elizabeth Jones, who remained his close spiritual companion, although they had surrendered the hope of marriage. On one occasion, when they were to meet and she was hindered from coming in time, Mr. Howells thought that she had failed at last and could no longer stand being seen with him, with his long, unkempt hair and beard. But she never failed once; she stood steadily with him right through.

But if at the beginning the world was affecting him, by the end it was he who was affecting the world, for people sensed the presence of God with him, and said so. Even some with no religious faith would take their hats off when they passed him in the streets. One old man used to tell people, "You mark my words: there goes a modern John the Baptist." An evidence of the effect he had on the district was seen later when a man who did not know his name simply asked the ticket collector at the station where "the man with the Holy Ghost" lived and was directed to Mr. Howells!

He himself said of the test, "In two weeks I had the victory and became dead to the influence of the world. It was as Paul said: 'The slight trouble [affliction] of the passing hour results in a solid glory past all comparison' (2 Cor. 4:17, Moffat). Oh the glory of that inward life! The three hours in the evening were a time spent in glory; it was nothing less than the Word being illuminated by the Holy Ghost. What perfect peace the Spirit gave me and what love for a lost soul!

"Up to that time I had always had fear of the searchings of the Holy Spirit. I was afraid of the new places of abiding because I could never refuse them, and while there is the least fear there is not perfect liberty. People may think they have no fear when really they have never been tested. I thought I would have no fear of going against the world and its opinions and that it was the easiest thing to be dead to it—but it was the greatest error I ever believed. I had to be pulled through inch by inch; it was the process of sanctification, when the self-nature and all its lusts had to be changed for the divine nature (Rom. 6:6; 2 Peter 1:4). Daily I decreased and He increased. Beyond all that, it was the third heaven with its eternal visions!"

After walking six months as a Nazarite, the Lord gave Rees the assurance that the intercession had been gained, and he came into wonderful liberty in the presence of God. He went straight to his mother and told her he was free, and that he could shave: at which she was so overjoyed that all she could say again and again was "Thank God!"

In the correspondence over the next few months between him and Mr. Gosset there were numerous references to this certainty in both their letters. The only immediate indications of the answer were that the son changed his way of life, signed the temperance pledge, left the army and went farming in Canada. It wasn't until twelve years later that Mr. Howells received the news of the full outcome of the intercession. A letter came from Mr. Edgar Faithfull, Secretary of the South Africa General Mission, written on August 3, 1921, from Cape Town. It said:

My dear Mr. Howells,

You will have heard of the death of Mr. John Gosset on March 12 last, after being ill for one week with pneumonia; his last words were, "The Lord has come." Mr. Pirouet received this news from his son, Ralph Gosset, who goes on to tell of his own conversion. (Did you say, *"Diolch Iddo"*?) An evangelist had been holding meetings which he and his wife went to. The man spoke on the Prodigal Son, and the words "he came to himself" stuck in Gosset's ears; the next day when ploughing they haunted him. A few days after, he and his wife stood up and testified in the meeting. This is great news, and I know you will be glad to hear it. I believe you gave time to definite prayer for him years ago, and had the assurance your prayer was heard. I believe Ralph Gosset is farming somewhere in Canada.

19

Uncle Dick's Healing

On the completion of the six months' intercession for Captain Gosset by Easter, 1910, Rees Howells was free to go back to a normal life. However, the Lord also gave him the offer of continuing in a hidden ministry for another four months to gain some other places of intercession, one being for the child widows of India whose sufferings were so great under the prevailing system. He chose to continue the hidden life because, he said, "the fellowship I had had with the Lord Himself surpassed all I ever had with man; also I had not finished going through the Bible with the Holy Spirit. The hardest thing in my life had become the sweetest."

The Lord then pointed out to Rees that these widows were living on only a handful of rice a day, and reminded him of the law of intercession, that before he could intercede for them he must live like them. So his diet was to be one meal of oats (porridge) every two days, "which the devil was apt to call pigs' food!" He was to give up bread, tea and sugar, and have a pennyworth of milk every two days, the whole costing less than 1s. 6d. a week.

The Lord also told him to leave home and live in rooms, as his mother could never have stood his living on so little. He knew fully that before it could be completed he would have to come to the position where he never wanted to change. Could the Holy Ghost so alter his taste that the food he was now to take would be as satisfying to him as the excellent food he was used to in his own home?

"What pangs of hunger I had," he said afterwards. "The Lord doesn't make it easy for you. He doesn't carry you through on eagle's wings, as it were. The victory is that you come up through it. I remember the feeling I had the first day, when I had no bread at all. I would have given anything for a crust. When you take the place of another, you take the suffering of another, you have to walk every inch of it.

"As every meal time came round, there was nothing for me. The wonder is that I didn't go under to it and give in. Only Ezekiel was my friend, and all I could say was, 'How did he do it?' " (Ezek. 4).

Nor must it be thought that intercession for Mr. Howells merely meant costly acts of obedience. With his own pangs, there went up a continual cry to God for the relief of the sufferers whose burden he was carrying.

He continued this for ten weeks, and it took ten days to get victory. He saw that the point of fasting is to bring the body into subjection to the Spirit. "Each fast, if carried out under the guidance of the Holy Spirit, means that our bodies become more equipped to carry burdens."

Rees began the day at 5 a.m., with no food all day, then sleeping on the floor, up again at 5 o'clock and going another day without food until 5 p.m. "I would have gone on like that all the days of my life to release those widows of India," he said. And when he did get victory, one meal in two days had become the same to him as having three meals a day. "I knew I was gaining a victory for the Lord," he said, "whereby He could release those widows."

It is a significant fact that with India's independence and new Constitution in 1949, at least a legal change has been made in the laws of inheritance for the benefit of widows, and that a new day has dawned in the general emancipation of women. Who knows what contribution this time of intercession made to this release, and indeed to the open doors throughout all India today for the spread of the gospel?

In this period of intercession, the final positions of fasting to which God called Rees were first to one meal every three days, and then to a total fast of fifteen days. By the seventh day of this, he said, "I was going on happily and wasn't touched by it. I was exactly the same the seventh day as on the first. I hadn't exhausted my strength at all and didn't feel the need for food." The Lord told him then that the intercession was gained and the fasting could finish, although he himself wanted to complete it.

During these final months of intercession, an incident took place which Mr. Howells always considered to be one of the greatest experiences of his life. Up on the Black Mountain, his invalid Uncle Dick was still living at Pentwyn, the grandparents' old home. On New Year's day, before going to visit him, Rees ran upstairs to his room. It was his habit before going out to ask the Lord to shelter him under the Blood and to lead him to anyone who needed his help.

That morning, quite unexpectedly, the Holy Spirit spoke to him: "It is the Father's will to restore your uncle." It seemed "too good to be true, and too great to believe"—that after all these thirty years his uncle should walk again as other men!

When he arrived at Pentwyn his uncle, who was always eagerly awaiting his weekly visit, asked him the usual question: "Anything new from the Lord?" "Yes," answered Mr. Howells, "and it is about you.'"

"About me!" was the surprised reply. "Have I done anything wrong?" "No, but the Lord has told me that it is His will to heal you."

We can only imagine what the news must have sounded like in the uncle's ears. All he could say was that he must go out and see the Lord about it. After a quarter of an hour in the little garden at the back, he returned with his face radiant. "Yes," he said, "I am to be healed in four and a half months, that will be on May 15."

If they had left it indefinite and not committed themselves to a date, it would have been much easier to make known the healing in public, but the point the Holy Spirit pressed home was that it was to be as much of a reality to them then as it would be to other people after it became a fact.

"Faith is the realization of things hoped for, the proof of things not seen" (Heb. 11:1, Rotherham). "This was not a case of the fight of faith," said Mr. Howells, "but of standing still and seeing the salvation of the Lord." The intercession had been gained in the long six months' battle for the tubercular woman, and "gaining it once meant gaining the position; it could be used in any other case the Holy Ghost wanted."

So the great news was made known that week, and soon became the talk of the district. Many pitied his uncle and said he had allowed himself to be led astray. Some came to ask why the Lord had said four and a half months, instead of a month or a week or a day. "Those things we did not understand and therefore did not try to explain," said Mr. Howells. "People are always asking 'why?' The only thing that could be said was that 'the spirits of the prophets are subject to the prophets,' and God gave that date."

Two weeks after it was made known, his uncle took a turn for the worse and was in bed for a month. People said that instead of being restored, he would be in the grave when the day came! Although he was very ill, the Holy Spirit warned them not to pray. If they did, their prayers would be prayers of doubt. Indeed the Lord had told his uncle, instead of praying for those ten hours a day, to prepare for the public work that would come to him after the healing.

Two weeks before the date of the healing, the Lord made it known to Mr. Howells that he was to leave home for a few months, and that after telling his uncle, he was not to visit him again until after the healing, because it was not God's will that any man should take praise from it. When he went down to Pentwyn his uncle asked, with the glory of the Lord on his face, "Has the Lord told you why He said four and a half months, and May 15? It will be Whitsunday. He is healing me in memory of Pentecost. God has told me that I am to be healed at 5 o'clock in the morning and I am to walk to chapel and back [a distance of three miles] for the first time in thirty years!"

As Mr. Howells had been going to visit his uncle every

week and now wasn't to go again, naturally the first thought that would come to everyone's mind was that he had run away and left his uncle in the lurch. "We laughed all day at the greatness of the divine plan," he said. "and our keynote for those last two weeks continued to be, 'Stand still and see the salvation of the Lord with you.' "

On the night before Whitsunday, his uncle was as bad as ever. Every night between 1 and 2 a.m. he had to get up, being unable to remain lying down, and he had to do it that morning. It was the last attack of the enemy, who whispered, "It is all up. You are just the same now as any other night, and you have only got three hours." One minute is quite long enough for the Lord. He went back to bed, and deep sleep came over him.

The next thing the uncle heard was the clock striking five, and he found himself perfectly restored. He called the family up, and there was such a solemn awe in the house that they were afraid to move, realizing that God Himself had done that great act that very hour.

When the time came to walk to church, the devil suggested that he should take a walking stick in case he needed a little support, to which he had to say, "Get thee behind me, Satan!"

He arrived at the church and they had "another cause for thanksgiving on that Thanksgiving Sunday." People from all parts of the district came the next day to see him, and the Welsh correspondent of *The Life of Faith*, the Rev. Wynne Evans, wrote an article in that paper about the wonderful healing.

Mr. Howells had invited two of his friends to come a distance of nearly ten miles to have tea with him that Whitsunday. They came through his uncle's district, actually passing the chapel he attended in the morning, but heard no news of his healing. Mr. Howells also had had no word. It was a day of testing; and the one topic at the tea table was: Had Uncle Dick been healed?

Although his best friend failed to hold out in his believing, God kept His servant steady until eleven o'clock on Monday night, when some of his friends called out under his window, "It was marvelous to see your uncle in chapel!" They thought he knew all about it, as they had sent word to him on Sunday; but the messenger entrusted the giving of the message to another, and it never arrived.

Mr. Howells' comment was, "If I had doubted, would I have rejoiced? The Lord will never give the witness unless we believe; and if we believe, we can afford the delay. To me there was something greater than the healing—it was the further confirmation that the position of intercession had been gained, and could be used in any case where God willed it."

His uncle was appointed a kind of honorary home missionary in the district, and during the next five years visited every house within a radius of three miles over and over again, and opened many a prayer meeting. He walked eighteen miles with his nephew one day, and never had a day's illness after his healing, until the Lord called him home, after telling him that his work on earth was done.

20

Called Out From Wage-Earning

It is hard to realize that throughout these three years of intense conflict and many triumphs in the Spirit, Rees Howells was working daily at one of the hardest jobs a man can do—down the mine, cutting coal. His was no sheltered, monastic life, but a walk in the Spirit right in the world, though never of it.

During the "spell" down in the mine—a period of ten to fifteen minutes when the men got accustomed to the darkness —if he was there, not an obscene word would pass their lips. The impression he made on many of those young fellows in the pit can best be gauged from an incident about ten years later, when he returned to Brynamman from the African mission field.

At a crowded meeting in his home church, the front row was filled with those same men, many of whom seldom came near a place of worship. One young miner, Mr. Tommy Howells, who had recently been converted, was so touched by the practical reality he saw in that life "full of faith and the Holy Ghost" that in that meeting their hearts became knit together as Jonathan's to David's, and for all the years that followed, "Tommy" became his devoted co-worker and prayer-partner.

But now there came a further call, which was to loosen him yet more from his old moorings. Rees was out on his favorite Black Mountain, where the silent spaces were so often the gate of heaven to him, and the Lord spoke to him. "For seven hours a day you are earning two shillings an hour," He said, "but you need not work for an earthly master any longer. Would you like to come out and give these seven hours a day to work for Me?"

Rees was standing on a small wooden bridge across a little stream, and the Lord asked him, "Will you give your word to Me that you won't look to another person to keep you? If so, put up your hand and repeat, 'I shall not take from a thread to a shoe latchet from any person, unless the Lord tells me.' "

Just as Abraham made that stand when he refused the spoils of war that were justly his, lest men should say his prosperity came from natural sources, so God was asking His servant to take this same stand for the rest of his life. On that bridge he raised his hand and made the solemn vow, adding, "I do believe You are able to keep me better than that mining company."

It was no mean stand of faith, because Mr. Howells had long since ceased that active ministry in the mission and among fellow Christians which might have led people to give to him. The moment he made this vow, the Lord drove home the reality of it to Rees by saying, "Remember this: you must never take a meal at home without paying for it, or your brothers could say they were keeping you." It was not that the family would have minded helping him, but the Lord was impressing on him that the real life of faith meant receiving all that he needed from God and being enabled to pay his way while using all his hours for God; and not being dependent upon any man, most of all his family.

Once again his obedience to God had to be proved at the price of wounding his mother. She had been so pleased that he was no longer living as a Nazarite and doing other "strange" things; surely now he would live a normal life. So when he told her of God's new word to him, she couldn't take it at first. It was a real conflict, and lasted some days. "What will your father say?" she asked. "If you pay, you will be like a lodger and not a son." But it was a vow to God, and as he said, God would change before he could break it. "If you will allow me to pay for my food, I will remain at home," Rees told her, "if not, I must leave this afternoon." He actually had to go out and try to arrange for lodgings before his mother agreed that he should pay her monthly.

The Lord then gave him a month's holiday, which he could spend in worshiping the Beloved of his heart. Each day was spent on the mountain where he never saw the face of man. They were not days of intercession or carrying burdens, but of living fellowship, lost in the presence of God. He often spoke of that month as one of the most precious of his life.

He started the month with one penny, and the Lord did not add anything to it; so as he climbed the mountain the first few days, the devil kept saying each morning, "You haven't had an answer to prayer yet." Then one morning, when he was passing through the iron gate, where he left houses and fields behind, the Lord said, "The moment you shut this gate behind you, don't allow the devil to speak to you again. You will not need a penny until the day you pay your mother."

"So I gave the enemy one hit," Rees said, "and told him that I wasn't going to pray a single prayer for money until the end of the month. I never doubted that the people I was working for would pay me on Saturdays, so why should I doubt God? I didn't pray a single prayer again, but lived to worship my heavenly Bridegroom."

On the last day of the month, about midday, the Lord told him to descend the mountain and go home; and as soon as he arrived, his father came in for lunch. The final test on his new call to a life of faith had come. "The manager says he has kept your job open, and you can take it again if you want to," his father informed him.

"What a foolish man! Why did he do that?" Rees exclaimed. "But if you don't mean to earn a living again," continued his father, "who is going to keep you?" "Don't you agree that if I am working for God, He can keep me as that last earthly master kept me?" asked Rees.

"But can you name one other person who lives this life?" his father asked. "George Muller," Rees answered. "But he is dead. Must you call the dead back to help you?" was the quick reply. "Well," Rees answered, "don't you believe the words of the Savior, 'Take neither purse nor scrip . . . the laborer is worthy of his hire'?" That quotation seemed to convince his father, who merely added, "I was only bringing you that message."

While he was speaking, the postman arrived with a letter for Rees. It was from Mr. Gosset, offering him a position in the London City Mission, and saying that he would have a salary of £100 a year. He added the words, "Those who preach the gospel should live of the gospel," and underlined them. Rees could see his father's countenance changing. He was plainly thinking, "How fortunate he is; everything turns out in his favor." "You see that?" he said to Rees. "Those who preach the gospel should live of the gospel!" "Certainly," Rees answered, "and those who preach faith should live by faith!" The victory was won, his father broke out laughing, and within half an hour the Lord had sent the deliverance he needed. It was a good beginning to forty years of praying and abundantly proving the Lord's prayer, "Give us this day our daily bread."

21

Madeira

Just at the time that Uncle Dick was healed a young man named Joe Evans, who had received a wonderful blessing in one of the first cottage meetings and was a great helper in the work, had a bad hemorrhage from the lungs. The doctors ordered him to a sanatorium. He came to ask Mr. Howells whether he should go. After waiting on God some days lest his judgment should be swayed by his natural desires, he told Joe to follow medical advice. It looked like a lapse of faith, but God had taught him that He steps in when natural remedies have failed. So he told Joe, "You will be quite safe in going to the sanatorium. Probably the Lord wants to show that medicine can't do it."

He was there for five months, but when he came out he had a high temperature and bad cough. The doctor gave him no hope, but ordered him to buy a tent and live up on the Black Mountain. "Do what the doctor tells you," said Mr. Howells again, "and if that fails, you will have a chance then for the Lord to heal you."

Often, when Mr. Howells visited him on the mountain, Joe would say jokingly, "After I have preached a full victory and you have gained that place of intercession, here I am in my tent like a flag on the top of this mountain, for all to see we have no faith for healing!"

Indeed, as Mr. Howells said, "If the Holy Ghost had not taught me that I was only to pray the prayers He gives, I would have taken up my friend's case long before that. It was a proof that, though the place of intercession was gained, I could only use it as led by the Spirit.''

Joe was on the mountain for over two months, but he was no better and the doctor said he could not possibly live through the winter unless he went to a tropical climate, such as Madeira. This was confirmed by a Swansea specialist. But when Joe's father heard it, he was roused against the doctor. The family was very poor, and he blamed the doctor because he had opened a door through which a rich man's son could go but his son could not.

That same day Mr. Howells received a gift of £320! "What did I want with £320," he said, "when I could live on twopence a day!" But the reason wasn't far to seek. It was "just like God." Here was the money for Joe! So Mr. Howells asked Joe's father, "If you were a moneyed man, would you send your son to the tropics?" "I should think I would!" he replied. "Well, I have the money and he can go."

The man broke down and cried. He was a stranger to the grace of God but, as Mr. Howells said, "He saw God's love making him equal to a rich man. I thought it was worth it all if only to reach him."

The next problem was how Joe could go to Madeira, when he was obviously not fit to travel alone. Mr. Howells hadn't thought of taking him himself, as already the Lord was beginning to show him plans for the future. But one night he couldn't sleep, and the Lord spoke to him. He asked him who was going to nurse Joe, and then added, "If you don't go with him yourself, don't allow him to go with anyone else. You must not ask anyone else to do what you can do yourself."

It was a test to the hilt. He knew what this might mean. He had dealt so much with tuberculars since the first case that it had given him a horror of the disease, and besides that there had been a great campaign against tuberculosis that year, showing the dangers of close contact with it.

Before mentioning it to anyone else, he told Miss Jones. He made plain to her what might be involved, and that in three months he might come back a tubercular. What would she say about it? She took two days to pray over it, and then told him it was settled. The Lord had asked her, "If Rees had been the tubercular and another person had offered to go with him, would she not have accepted that? And does not the Word say, 'Do to others as you would that they should do to you'?" On that she came through.

So Joe and he started for the island of Madeira in the summer of 1910. On arrival, the missionary at Funchal, to whom Mr. Howells had an introduction, came to meet them. He noticed at once that Joe was in an advanced stage of the disease, and asked if they had been advised to come by more than one medical man. He then inquired which hotel they would prefer, the English being 7s. 6d. a day and the Portuguese 4s. 2d. The Lord had already told Mr. Howells to take his usual place of abiding and only use money on essentials, so they decided on the Portuguese hotel.

To Mr. Howells "the fare was first class, after living on one meal every two days," but it was not to be for long. The Portuguese food did not suit Joe, and by the third day he was very upset. So Mr. Howells told him to rest quietly while he went out in the country and spent a time with the Lord. Here the Lord showed him what to do.

He had a right to go up to 8s. 4d. a day, the cost of two at the hotel, so he could put Joe at the English hotel for 7s. 6d. and live himself on the remaining 10d.

When the missionary heard this, he said it was impossible to sleep in Madeira for 1s. a night, and much less live on it, but he had a suggestion to make. Mr. Howells could use the Sailors' Rest, the basement of the mission house. He might have offered him a room in the mission house, which would have seemed the kinder thing to do, but God was in the offer, and He had a special purpose in it.

This Sailors' Rest was a large building, with room for over a dozen people, "but it had not been occupied for months," said Mr. Howells, "except by the creatures that live in empty places in the tropics. I experienced a little of what Pharoah and his people went through in the third and fourth plagues in Egypt!

"There was no sleep the first night, from fightings without and fears within! Things came to a climax at breakfast the next morning. The little box of Quaker oats, the bread and cheese, had others besides myself to share them, and they were busy at their breakfast when I went to prepare mine! I thought I had the same right to complain as Peter—about creeping things, and I began to take thoughts into my mind against the missionary. I wouldn't usually do that for anything. I took care of my mind; but this began to be magnified in me and I found something in me which prevented me from loving him.

"I was tired and I felt as if life wasn't worth living. I felt more like a man than a man with the Holy Ghost living in him. I wanted to cry, but the Lord said, 'Before you cry, I want to speak to you. Haven't you preached on James Gilmour in Mongolia living on 2d. a day? Didn't you preach on Ezekiel and the way he lived?' I asked the Lord to forgive me, but He said, 'It must be in you. I brought you to Madeira, to this place, to show you the difference between My love and yours; and to show you that there is something in your nature that I need to rid you of.

" 'The Savior loved you when you treated Him worse than the missionary has treated you. When He was on earth, He had a position you haven't allowed Me to come up to in you—loving others who do something against you, loving people who give their second or third best, just as if they had given you the very best.'

"I praised God for finding this out in me. I was to love the missionary, not for what he gave me but because I couldn't help loving him. I could see the root of the Savior's nature was love, and if the root of mine was love, nothing the missionary did could affect me. I saw it in a flash, and went on my knees, and asked the Holy Spirit not to move me from that place till I came through. Supposing I had remained blind and a fool, and gone on preaching the Sermon on the Mount with this in my nature! If ever I loved the Savior, it was then. I saw Him loving those who put Him to death—and there are no limits to that love.

"I went out to the hills of Madeira that day and saw His beauty and worshiped Him. I lost sight of my friend, and lived with the Savior who is perfect, holy. I saw what it would be when I gained the position: the Holy Ghost in me with a perfect love, perfect forgiveness and perfect mercy towards others. You might think I would gain it in an hour. A person might say, 'You could have forgiven!' Yes, perhaps an imitation forgiveness and the thing coming back to you again. You never really forgive until you become like the Savior and can forgive like Him. Several times I thought it was real and that I loved the missionary, until I saw him. Then other feelings would return!

"But in six weeks I had changed, as much as a drunkard is changed when he sees what the Savior has done for him. I changed altogether. What a life He brought me into! Oh, that perfect love! The proof of it was when I met the local evangelist next day. He had not talked much with me before, but this morning he said, 'Where do you live?' 'In the mission house,' I replied. 'In the house?' he asked. I said to myself, 'You devil!' I could see Satan behind him. 'In the Sailors' Rest?' he continued. 'Yes,' I answered. 'Do you call that Christianity in your country, putting you in a place like that?' he exclaimed. (What if he had asked me that a few days before!)

"I answered him by asking another question: 'Do you pay for your electric light and laundry?' 'Yes,' he said. 'They're very expensive.' 'Well, I get mine free. That's Christianity. That's what the missionary had done for me!' Oh, the freedom! Oh, the victory! After that, I never lived in any place which God filled more than the Sailors' Rest. There was more fellowship in an hour there than in all the time at the hotel with its good meals. I knew the difference between my living in the Sailors' Rest and God living there."

Meanwhile, after two months in the English hotel, Joe was showing no signs of improvement. One day he broke down completely: he thought he was dying, and a longing for home and the old country came over him. It was a dark moment and Mr. Howells felt he must take a stand. "Do you think the Lord brought you out here and would allow you to die, without revealing His will to us?" he asked him and added, "This sickness is not unto death, but for the glory of God." As they parted by the little train which took Mr. Howells down the mountain, Joe burst out crying. It was difficult to go for Mr. Howells was afraid he might get a hemmorhage in the night, and his tears moved him.

"As I entered the little train," he said, "I heard that Voice which I know as really as a child knows his father's voice. It said, 'A month today Joe will be restored.' The glory of God came down on the train. It was such that the people turned round and seemed to notice something."

On arriving at the Sailors' Rest he sat down immediately and wrote three letters home: to his family, to Joe's father, and to Miss Jones, saying that in a month's time they would be back. On that day, "when everything of nature and medicine had failed," the Lord showed him that "a higher law was going to operate."

The next morning he returned to Reid's hotel to break the news to Joe. Rees first asked him, in his mischievous way, what prospects he now had for the future; to which Joe mournfully replied, "Nothing but the grave." Joe had promised not to grumble when he was moved to the English hotel, so he was resigned to God's will! Mr. Howells then reminded him of God's goodness to him in the sanatorium, in the open-air treatment, and in Madeira, and quietly added: "But He has kept the best wine until now; God is going to heal you in a month!"

The tears started to flow. "It was like a fountain opened," said Mr. Howells, "and they flowed for two or three days. It seemed too good to believe that he was going home to see his friends. He said he had believed my uncle's case, but to believe for himself was another matter. However, in a day or two he had really grasped it."

Mr. Howells met the missionary's wife that night, and as usual she asked after his friend. "He is very ill," was the answer, "but the Lord has told me He is going to heal him in a month." It seemed an incredible statement to her, and she exclaimed, "How can you say such a thing? You know it can never happen, when both his lungs are nearly gone. It has never happened before!" "It has never happened because of unbelief," Rees replied, "but the Lord has told me He is going to heal Joe. We shall be returning home in a month's time."

The next morning he met the missionary. He had heard from his wife of their conversation, and he said to him, "I hear you are returning in a month! You came out for the winter, and here you are going back in mid-winter with a tubercular. Are you willing to try a specialist?" "Certainly," replied Mr. Howells. "I have £200, and I am ready to try all that medicine can do, and will do anything the specialist says."

He explained to the missionary that he had no conflict with medicine, and that God doesn't step in with a spiritual law till the end of the law of nature has been reached, and he asked him, "If the specialist gives him up, then when he is healed will you believe it is God who has done it?" "I will," he replied with tears in his eyes, "I have never heard anything more reasonable."

The missionary made it known in all the hotels in Madeira. He also was very surprised at the mention of the £200. He couldn't understand why Mr. Howells lived in the Sailors' Rest if he had all that money!

The specialist gave Joe a thorough examination, and said he was in a critical condition, and was about to have another hemorrhage. He told Mr. Howells not to let him out of his sight, and that the best thing would be to return home. "So we were both satisfied that the law of nature was at an end," commented Mr. Howells.

When the letter arrived home in Brynamman, saying that Joe was to be healed in a month, his mother showed it to the doctor who had first advised Joe to go to the sanatorium. He laughed when he read it, and said it was impossible, but added that if it became a fact, he would become a believer that day.

Mr. Howells had promised the specialist he would keep

near Joe, so he joined him at the hotel. "It was a month's holiday," he said, "because this case needed no prayer. The Lord had said he would be healed, so we trusted His word, and were as happy as birds. Many in Funchal came to know about it, and were watching for the outcome with keen interest."

The week before the healing, they booked their passages and made all preparations for leaving. Rees Howells also reminded Joe that Uncle Dick had had the exact time of healing given to him, and suggested that Joe should go to the Lord and ask the time that he was to be healed on the Saturday morning, so that he himself should have a part in it. He came back laughing, saying that he had 3 a.m. and 6 a.m., but he knew that the former came from the devil, because it was too early, so he took the latter! They agreed to send a cable home to Joe's father on the day of the healing.

"It was a very exciting time the day before," said Rees. "I had told him to come into my bedroom at six o'clock the next morning, and bring the news to me. When we shook hands to part for the night, he said, 'I am very nervous, when I think I am going to bed for the last time with this tuberculosis on me.'

"As for myself, I could hardly sleep all night for joy and excitement, but it was a solemn time, especially between five and six in the morning, waiting for the expected hour to come. But at six o'clock there was no sign of Joe. I called to him, and here he came with his rug over his head and sat at the foot of my bed with his countenance down, and said, 'There is no change in me; I am exactly the same as I was yesterday!'

"At once the Holy Ghost said to me, 'Are you sending the cable?' I told Joe to go back and pray for me. He couldn't understand why he should do that—he thought he was the one who needed prayer! I then went back to the Lord, and asked Him what was the cause of the delay. 'If I tell you he is restored,' He said, 'will you send the cable? If you take the healing from Me against what you can see and what your friend says, you will have gained a higher position than in your uncle's healing.' Here was a very keen point.

"I knew what it meant to send that cable to the place where

my uncle was healed. Everyone would say, if I failed in this, that my uncle's healing was chance. Only a real faith in God could make me do it. The Lord brought to my mind the case of the centurion's servant. Would I believe God's word against what I could see?

"After wrestling for an hour, I came right through to sending it simply on the word of God, before the actual healing took place. I went up to the post office before eight o'clock that morning and cabled the one word: *Victory*. After the cable had gone I found my hands were dripping with perspiration.

"The next day was Sunday, and at noon we were both sitting out in front of the hotel waiting for lunchtime when the Lord came down on Joe like a shower of rain, and he was healed on the spot. He told me at once, and was dancing with joy. He asked me to run a race with him, and we did, until he outran me. He was like Elijah running before Ahab—it seemed that all the power had gone to his legs! In our joy we broke the Sabbath by running races! It was joy unspeakable, not only the healing, but the victory of faith. We both attended the missionary's meeting that afternoon. It was the first Joe had been in for twelve months. The victory was wonderful, as the missionary made known the healing in public."

Two days later they left Madeira for home. They had a great send-off from the hotel by many whom the Lord had blessed, and there was a great parting scene with the missionary and his family.

They arrived home on a Saturday, and the next day the doctor came to the house and asked Joe if he had any objection to being examined. Joe was quite willing, and after the examination, the doctor said, "It is wonderful, wonderful. I can't find a trace of the disease in him!"

The doctor went to chapel that Sunday for the first time since he had come to the district. Some months after, when another tubercular went to him, he said to him, "Look here, a doctor can't do anything for you; go and try the Lord!" The young man looked at him, as if he was making fun, but he repeated it: "I mean it, go and try the Lord!"

After the healing, the reality of the intercessory path that lay behind this victory was tested to the farthest point. Joe entered the ministry, for which he had previously felt a call; but soon after they got back from Madeira, Mr. Howells found himself coughing up blood. He felt sure that in his close association with Joe, he had taken the disease. He found his inward peace undisturbed, and he had no regrets at what had been done. Actually after several days it was found that the trouble was nothing serious, but he had proved to his own heart that his surrender had been real.

22

Marriage and Missionary Call

Very soon after his return from Madeira, Rees Howells married Elizabeth Hannah Jones, who also came from Brynamman. Their wedding took place on December 21, 1910. They had known each other from childhood. After months of deep conviction, she had been born again in the Welsh Revival. Later she became one of the band of helpers in the village and gradually the Lord had drawn them together, until they wondered if it were God's will for them to marry and make a home for the tramps.

Soon after, however, they were led in the opposite direction —to give up their marriage, not knowing whether it would ever be restored to them. Only now, three years later, did the Lord's word come that their lives should be united in His service. Wholly one with him in outlook, Mrs. Howells became a God-given helpmeet to her husband and an unfailing co-worker, always sharing the burdens in the Spirit.

A handsome gift was received from America for the wedding expenses. Part of it was spent in buying necessities, and part kept for the time of the wedding. A week before the event, however, a person in great need came to Mr. Howells for help. In the life of faith, he always maintained the principle "first need, first claim"; and this man's need came a week before theirs. So he gave him the money, feeling sure the Lord would supply.

But by the day before the wedding, nothing had come. "I

told the Lord," he said, "that if it was any other day, I would not mind; but we could *never* do without on that day, as we had invited my sister and brother-in-law to accompany us in the morning, and we were to catch the train before the first post. The evening came, and I didn't have a single penny! It was an occasion when one could doubt the Lord, but He had never failed, and late that night the deliverance came. There was great value in it! That was our start together in a life of faith!"

A few months later he went to America with a friend and began to preach again. He visited many old acquaintances, especially in the town where he had been converted. After three months they returned, and it was not long before the Holy Ghost revealed to him that he was to start attending chapel again. It was a strange feeling after being so long in the mission, and then living a hidden life. He and Elizabeth had not been in the chapel for over five years.

The next point was, to which should they go? He used to be a member of the Congregational Church, and she a Baptist. As they sought the Lord's guidance they were led to a small Congregational chapel which had no minister at the time.

This move, however, was more puzzling to the believers than even the hidden life had been, for after the Revival there had been some estrangement between those who had been blessed and the chapels. Many had left and started missions. Rees' eldest brother John, for instance, who was always held in highest respect by the family, was converted in the Revival while a deacon in one of the chapels and he, with some friends, was later responsible for building the Gospel Hall in Brynamman, which is still an evangelistic center in the town.

As time went on, the distance between the missions and chapels had often grown wider, although in churches where the ministers had been blessed in the Revival, the converts remained and helped them. So when the people heard that Rees had gone back to the chapel, it was looked upon as a sign of backsliding, especially as the one he began to attend was within a mile of the mission.

From the first he started taking part in the meetings, and there was a move of the Spirit. Then one Sunday, when on the way to service, God told him that he was to enter the ministry! Rees went straight home and asked his wife, "Did you know you had married a minister?" He said nothing of this to the people.

Then one night the elders asked him if he would like to enter the ministry, and after a church meeting Rees was accepted and preached his first sermon. A call to the ministry meant training, so together with his wife's brother he began to attend the theological college at Carmarthen.

"In my preaching at that time," he remembered, "I never touched on intercession or on my past life, any more than the Apostle spoke of his years in Arabia. I was called to preach the simple gospel, and I kept just to that. What a privilege it was to stand in the pulpit and in the power of the Holy Ghost proclaim the unsearchable riches of Christ!

"The Lord allowed me to go back and live a most natural life. I was always thankful to Him for letting me have the privilege of preaching to the multitudes in many chapels in the district. There is no glory like that of proclaiming the cross. I was called to preach more about eternal life than about the divine Person of the Holy Ghost, as there are a great many in our country who believe in the atonement and resurrection but have no assurance that they have passed from death unto life.

"From the time I began to preach, there was no further place of intercession gained, because all my hours and thoughts were given to that work." But he was the same Rees Howells. One day in Carmarthen, he and a fellow-student passed a thinly clad tramp shivering with the cold. Mr. Howells at once took off his overcoat and gave it to him.

Then, in the midst of all this, God called again. The Howells had a burden of prayer for some missionary friends in West Africa: Mr. and Mrs. Stober of the Angola Evangelical Mission. Rees and Elizabeth felt they should help them in some way, and while they were asking the Lord about it, they read in their magazine that a little girl, Edith, had been born to the

Stobers. Mr. Howells knew West Africa was no climate for children, so he told his wife that this would be a good chance to help them—they could take the little girl while the parents were in Africa.

It was a real test: Mrs. Howells would be tied at home, yet the child would never become theirs. She made the decision. "If they give their lives for Africa," she said, "I will give mine for the child." They wrote and told the Stobers, but the answer came that they were soon coming home and could then talk it over.

"I met my friend Stober at the Llandrindod Convention," said Mr. Howells. "He did not say anything for the first few days, and it wasn't until I was on my way to the missionary meeting that he told me how thankful he and his wife were for the offer we had made, but that they were not wanting to leave Edith just then.

"I walked straight into the meeting, and there I saw a vision of Africa! Mrs. Albert Head was speaking on behalf of the South Africa General Mission, and pleading for a married couple to take the place of Mr. and Mrs. Edgar Faithfull, as he was becoming the home secretary. I had heard many people speaking on the need of the mission field, but I never 'saw' the heathen in their need until that afternoon. The Lord gave me a vision of them, and they stood before me as sheep without a shepherd."

Rees returned home on Saturday and told Elizabeth, especially about the married couple. That night they prayed for this couple, and could not stop praying for a long time. When they did stop, they could not sleep; and before the morning the Lord had said, "I will answer the prayer through you. I will send you both out there."

"It was the greatest surprise of our lives," said Rees. "We thought we had a vision of the Africans in order to burden us to pray for someone else to go, but with the Lord we can only push others as far as we are willing to be pushed ourselves. There were a thousand and one hindrances, but the Lord would take no excuses—where there's a will, there's a way!"

The greatest problem was that a little boy had been born to them. At the time they had offered to adopt Edith, they had no child. "We had told each other that those missionaries ought to give the child up and devote all their time to the work," said Mr. Howells, "but we little thought that we were preparing a trap for ourselves; what we thought others should do, we were now called to do!"

Months before their little boy was born, the Lord told them to call his name Samuel. There was no Samuel in the family; it was given them, just as the name of John was given to Zacharias. There were several similarities in his life to the one he was named after: one being that Mrs. Howells' name was Hannah, and she too was now to put her son on the altar of sacrifice.

"It was our first test on the call, and the greatest," said Mr. Howells, who tells the story in his own words. "The Savior had said, 'Anyone who loves son or daughter more than Me is not worthy of Me,' and now the Holy Ghost said to us, 'You must prove to Me that you love the souls of the Africans who are to live for eternity more than you love your own son.'

"*Does He really mean it?* I wondered. Yes, He meant it, just as He told Abraham to take his only son up the mountain and offer him as a whole burnt offering. Many a time I had preached about Abraham giving up Isaac, and had emphasized the words, 'Take now thy son, thine only son, whom thou lovest.' How little had I realized what that had meant to him!

"I knew what it was to give my life, but to give another's life away was as different as two things could be. God had given us Samuel's name before he was born, and I knew He had a purpose for his life, and this was our test. God said, 'If you give him up, you can never claim him again.' Not once has it ever dawned on us since then that Samuel was ours.

"We were to surrender him as really as God surrendered His own Son, and Abraham his son. Unless your surrender is real and up to the standard, you will break down long before the end. It wasn't a question of leaving Samuel behind, and then that he should call our attention back to himself; no thought of Samuel was to bring us back to this country.

"The time came for my wife to take a course of Bible training. We did not know what place the Lord would open for little Samuel. We left it entirely in the hands of the Lord; we wouldn't have dared to interfere, or we could have made the greatest mistake.

"A few weeks before the time for us to leave I was sent for by my uncle, a brother of the one who was healed; his wife was the headmistress in the country school where they lived in Garnant, near Ammanford. He asked if we were taking Samuel with us. I said, 'No.' 'Where is he going to?' I said I didn't know. 'Well,' he said, 'he is to come here.' They had never seen him, although they lived within three or four miles, but he said that a few nights before, something came over them about him, and they wanted to nurse him while we were away. In a couple of days they were coming up to see him.

"Walking home that day to tell my wife was more than one could bear. Although we had given him up in our hearts, when the Lord actually opened a door for him, it was like pulling one's heart to pieces. But before I had reached home, I had enough victory to control myself; it would have been no use for me to show my wife that I was giving way.

"When I arrived home she was playing with Samuel. I thought I had never seen him as he was that night, and for a time I could not break the news. But I took courage and told her.

"The scene that followed can better be imagined than described, and we were glad we only had to go through it once in a lifetime. We proved that night that Africa was going to cost us something. We were coming up to the victory by degrees; the process was slow and hard. Because it was going to be an intercession, one had to walk every inch.

"My uncle and aunt came up, and they had never seen a child like him! Without a doubt the Lord had put a father's and mother's love in their hearts toward him. The first thing they did was to invite my sister to be his nurse. It was like Miriam and Moses.

"The morning came when my sister arrived to fetch him. I

think in eternity we shall look back on what we went through then, giving our best to the Lord. We knew what it was to give money, health, and many other things, but this was the hardest test.

"The devil was not quiet that morning. He said I was the hardest man in the world to give my little child up. The worst of all was to enter into the feelings of my wife, preparing his clothes, etc. His going out was more than emptying the house —he emptied our hearts too.

"When I came home that night, I asked my wife, 'How did you get through?' She said she went into the garden and wept, and thought to herself, 'I have been singing that hymn many a time:

But we never can prove the delights of His love,
Until all on the altar we lay,

and this morning I have to prove it.' But then the Lord told me, 'Measure it with Calvary.' And with those words she came through.

"In praying together afterwards, the Lord showed me the reward. He said to us, 'For everything you give up for Me, there is the hundredfold; and on this you can claim 10,000 souls in Africa,' and we believed it."

After Mr. and Mrs. Howells left for Africa, Samuel became so completely a son to Mr. and Mrs. Rees that his name was changed to Samuel Rees. He grew up with them and later went to Oxford University where he graduated. It was with him literally, as with Samuel of old, that he seemed set apart for the Lord and served Him from his youth up. He accepted Christ as his personal Savior at the age of twelve. His adopted parents wanted him to become a doctor, but Samuel felt the Lord's call to the ministry. After his University course he came back to join his own father (with his foster parents' loving consent) although Mr. and Mrs. Howells never raised one finger to draw him in their direction. It was God who sent him back to them.

Samuel became Assistant Director of the Bible College of which, after his father's home call, he became Director, and was once again known to everybody by the name of Samuel

Rees Howells. How perfectly the Lord fulfilled the promises given to his father and mother even before his birth, and how abundantly the Lord honored the sacrifice made by his parents in giving him up and the love and care showered on him by his foster parents.

23

Standing in the Queue

Meanwhile Mr. Howells had written to Mr. Albert Head, who was chairman of the South Africa General Mission, as well as being chairman of the Keswick and Llandrindod Conventions, and offered for the mission field. He told him about the healing of his uncle and Joe. Mr. Howells received a letter from Mr. Head asking him to come up to London and meet the Council of the mission, and to bring Joe with him.

The morning they left for London, he and Mrs. Howells only had £2, and she needed money that very day. But as usual, 'First need, first claim.' As he was going before the post arrived, he had the claim on the money, and he comforted his wife by saying that more would be sure to come in the post!

He and Joe arrived in London with only five shillings, having bought one-way fares. Mr. Howells met the Council the next evening, and he and Mrs. Howells were accepted for the field. A meeting had been arranged for him the following day by Mr. Head, where he was to speak on intercession. The Lord blessed, and when he left the day after, Mr. Head shook hands with him and said, "The Lord has been speaking to me through you. I have never 'kept' a missionary before, but God has told me to keep you as my missionary. No one else is to support you, and while you are preaching in Africa, I will share in the harvest!"

Before they took their return train, they had lunch with some friends and, as they left, an envelope was placed into Mr. Howells' hand. When he opened it at Paddington, there were five golden sovereigns inside. They had arrived with five shillings, but were leaving with five pounds! "The Lord has only done for us what He did with the water that was turned into wine," Joe remarked. "He has just changed the color!" They had a praise meeting when they arrived home with Mrs. Howells telling how the £2 came half an hour after he had left. "There is nothing in the world better for strengthening one's faith than testings!" was Mr. Howells' comment.

Later, they both left for Scotland, where Mrs. Howells was to take a year's training in the Faith Mission. Shortly afterwards, he left her there and went on to London for a nine month medical course at Livingstone College. Here again there were many trials of faith, and deliverances.

His special friend at the College, with whom he had close fellowship in the Spirit, was Mr. Harold St. John of the Brethren, who became well known later as a Bible teacher. They used to get up at five o'clock each morning to wait on God, knocking on the wall between them to wake each other. Meanwhile, Mr. Howells never once had to send her anything. "We were in the school of faith," he said, "and there is nothing to be compared with having to be delivered to keep you abiding; you will never do it without."

On one occasion he only had a few days in which to get £20. This was needed for Mrs. Howells' admission to a maternity course in the City Road Hospital, for which she was coming down to London. There was another student, a Cambridge graduate, who had been saying openly that he had never prayed a prayer that had brought a direct, definite answer. So Mr. Howells invited him to join in this prayer for £20. He had never heard of praying for money like that and expecting it to come. They were to pray for two hours one afternoon, each in his own room. The young man was exhausted at the end of it! He had never known time to go so slowly; he said the two hours were like two months!

Mr. Howells did not pray through in the afternoon, so he suggested that they should go back for a further two hours in the evening. "What!" exclaimed his friend, "Four months' hard labor for £20!'' However, he agreed to try again if Mr. Howells thought he could be of any help. Before the end of this second period of prayer, however, Mr. Howells went to the young man's room and said, "You don't need to pray any more; I am through." "Have you got the money?" he asked. "No, but I have got the faith, and the money will come."

Late that night they were taking a walk together when this student suddenly stopped, leaned against a fence, and roared with laughter. "What are you laughing at?" Mr. Howells asked. "I was just thinking of the chap who will have to give that £20." He had seen it. Two days later Mr. Howells received two £10 notes. What a blessing it was when he went to his friend's room and held them up for him to see! It became quite a habit of the Principal of the College to invite Mr. Howells in for tea whenever he had any special visitors, and ask him to relate some of his experiences of faith.

Some people wondered why Mr. Howells studied medicine after the Lord had given him such wonderful cases of healing. But the point was, as has already been mentioned, that he never was opposed to medicine. The principle that he had found in a life of intercession was that "man's extremity is God's opportunity," and most of the cases for which he had prayed for healing were ones where medicine had failed.

Commenting on this, Mr. Howells said that he had only refused to give medicine in one case, and that was the time when Samuel was born and his wife was gravely ill. The Lord had told him she was not to take medicine. "What a test it was!" he remembered. "It was a fight of faith for me and a fight with death for her. I never shook in my position. The one thing I knew was that the Lord *told* me. I said to my wife, 'You are not to take medicine, and you are not to die.' At our extremity, in our reading one morning, the words 'Have faith in God' stood out in golden letters. We believed, and from that moment she began to get well."

On the general subject of medicine and faith, Mr. Howells said: "To tell other people not to take medicine, when we are not sure of our guidance, is nothing less than tragedy, if they die. But I know of cases where people were guided not to take medicine and had victory all through their lives. One was Lord Radstock, who gave me many instances of how the Lord had honored faith. Another was A. B. Simpson, the founder of the Christian and Missionary Alliance, who proved over and over again that there is healing in the Blood. In cases of giving medicine, it depends wholly on guidance; if the Holy Ghost leads a person not to give it, He will be sure to make up for it.

"Elizabeth and I were both guided to take a course in nursing and medicine, and the proof was that the Lord had to answer prayer to enable us to do so. After we had finished our training in Edinburgh and London, the Lord opened the way for me to be a dispenser with a doctor for six months, and my wife to take a maternity course, both of which proved most useful on the mission field."

About a week before they sailed, they received money from the mission to pay their expenses to London, but they needed some things to complete their outfit, and once again the rule was applied—first need, first claim.

"There is always a tendency to keep money, so as to get out of God's testings," said Mr. Howells, "and we tried our best to do it this time! Anyway, we had to spend the money, and all the people of the place thought we were well supplied. So we were, up to that week, and we thought money would be sure to come the day before we were to leave for London; but the last post came and no money, and our train was leaving before the post next morning. We thought it would be very hard to say good-bye to my uncle and aunt and little Samuel, but the burden for the train money made the parting a little easier! That is often the way with the Lord; when we have a very hard thing to do, He will burden us in another way to make the former one easier!

"Next morning it was not so hard to part with our parents, because we had to walk to the station without the money! We felt sure that it would come on the station platform, but no, the time came for the train to leave. What were we to do? There was only one thing possible. We still had ten shillings, and we must go as far as we could with it; then our extremity would be God's opportunity. We had to change trains at Llanelly Station, about twenty miles from our home, and wait there a couple of hours; so without letting anyone know, we only booked as far as that.

"There were many people at our home station wishing us all the good things, but what we needed was money to go to London! Many also came as far as Llanelly, singing all the way. The thought that came to me was, 'I'd sing better if I had the money!'

"We went out to breakfast with some friends at Llanelly, and then walked back to the station still not delivered; and now the time for the train had come. The Spirit then spoke to me and said, 'If you had money, what would you do?' 'Take my place in the queue at the booking office,' I said. 'Well, are you not preaching that My promises are equal to current coin? You had better take your place in the queue.' So there was nothing I could do except obey.

"There were about a dozen people before me. There they were passing by the booking office one by one. The devil kept telling me, 'Now you have only a few people in front of you, and when your turn comes, you will have to walk through. You have preached much about Moses with the Red Sea in front and the Egyptians behind, but now *you* are the one who is shut in.' 'Yes, shut in,' I answered, 'but like Moses, I'll be gloriously led out!'

"When there were only two before me, a man stepped out of the crowd and said, 'I'm sorry I can't wait any longer, but I must open my shop.' He said good-bye and put thirty shillings in my hand! It was most glorious, and only a foretaste of what the Lord would do in Africa, if we would obey. After I had the tickets, the people who came with us to the train began to give gifts to us, but the Lord had held them back until we had been tested. We were singing all the way to London!"

On their arrival, Mr. Head asked them to breakfast the next morning. He then told them that he had £50 for them, but he didn't post it. "Thank God, you didn't," said Mr.

Howells, adding to himself, "I wouldn't have been without the test in the queue for anything."

They had all their outfit except three things: a watch, a fountain pen, and a raincoat each. They had never mentioned these things to anyone, but at breakfast Mr. Head asked, "What kind of watches have you?" and told them that his son, Alfred, wanted to give them a watch each. He then asked, "Have you prepared for the rainy seasons in Africa? Have you got good raincoats?" When they said they hadn't, he told them to go and get one each, and wrote down an address on a card, saying that they were to get them at his expense. After writing the address, he asked, "Have you seen this kind of fountain pen?" "No," they replied. "You must take one each with you," he said. The three things they had named to the Lord, he named to them!

Mr. Head asked them to come to breakfast the following morning again and take prayers. He suggested that Mr. Howells should tell the servants a little of his experiences of faith. "You used to have a life of faith, some time ago, didn't you?" he asked. "Yes, and quite recently too," answered Mr. Howells, and told them about standing in the queue. Mr. Head could hardly breathe, waiting to hear how he got out of it. "I have never heard anything like it," he exclaimed. But Mr. Howells told them he hadn't finished yet, and that what had happened at Corrie Lodge the previous day in that very room was better still, and he told them the story of the watches, raincoats, and fountain pens. "I prefer this to £1,000," said Mr. Head, "to know that the Lord can guide me like this in my giving."

So they left England on July 10, 1915, after a glorious victory, knowing that the One who had called them into this life was able to deliver in all circumstances.

24

Revivals in Africa

The South Africa General Mission had been founded in 1889 to take the gospel into the many unevangelized areas of South Africa, the first President of the Mission being the Rev. Andrew Murray. When Mr. and Mrs. Howells joined it, the Mission had 170 European and African workers in twenty-five stations, reaching as far north as the southern frontier of the Belgian Congo, and east and west into untouched parts of the Portuguese territories of Angola and Mozambique. The Howells were sent to the Rusitu Mission Station in Gazaland, near the border of Portuguese East Africa. They joined Mr. and Mrs. Hatch who had labored there for several years and who, with others who had preceded them, had laid a firm foundation and paid a real price in taking the gospel to these people.

Mr. and Mrs. Hatch had recently been studying the subject of the Lord's Second Coming and, giving time to the Word of God and prayer, longed for a deeper blessing in their own souls in order that fuller blessing might come to their people. When, therefore, the Howells arrived, there was already preparation of heart for a work of the Holy Spirit.

The natural thing for new recruits to the mission field is to spend a considerable period in language study, acclimatization and the general getting used to life in a new country. But the people had already heard that Mr. and Mrs. Howells came from the land where the Revival had been, and straightway asked them if they had brought that blessing with them. Mr.

Howells told them that the Source of all revival is the Holy Ghost, and that He could do among them what He had done in Wales. They asked him to preach about it (of course by interpretation). Since they had no word in their language for revival he told them about Pentecost: that it was God who had come down then, moving upon the hearts of men and women, and had swept multitudes into the Kingdom, and that He would do the same with them if they were willing to repent.

In the meetings that Mr. Howells took he continued to speak to them about revival, and in six weeks the Spirit began to move upon the Christians. On Friday evening, when about a dozen of them had gathered in the Howells' house, Mrs. Howells taught them the chorus, "Lord, send a revival, and let it begin in me." The Spirit was upon them as they sang, and they continued the singing the next days in their gardens and elsewhere. As Mr. Howells listened to them, he recognized a sound he had heard in the Welsh Revival. "You know it when you hear it," he said, "but you can't make it; and by the following Thursday, I was singing it too. There was something about it which changed you, and brought you into the stillness of God."

That evening, as their custom was each Thursday, the four missionaries met together for Bible reading and prayer. While they were on their knees, the Lord spoke to Mr. Howells, telling him that their prayer was heard and the revival was coming. He called them all to rise; there was no need of further prayer: the Holy Ghost was coming down to give a Pentecost in their district.

So great was the power of God's Word that every moment after that they expected the break. At every knock on the door they felt sure it was someone coming to tell them that the Holy Ghost had come. They waited thus for two days, and on Sunday—He came! We have Mr. Howells' own account of the days that followed:

"The Sunday was October 10—my birthday—and as I preached in the morning, you could feel the Spirit coming on the congregation. In the evening, down He came. I shall never forget it. He came upon a young girl, Kufase by name, who had fasted for three days under conviction that she was not ready for the Lord's coming. As she prayed she broke down crying, and within five minutes the whole congregation were on their faces crying to God. Like lightning and thunder the power came down. I had never seen this, even in the Welsh Revival. I had only heard about it with Finney and others. Heaven had opened, and there was no room to contain the blessing.

"I lost myself in the Spirit and prayed as much as they did. All I could say was, 'He has come!' We went on until late in the night; we couldn't stop the meeting. What He told me before I went to Africa was actually taking place, and that within six weeks. You can never describe those meetings when the Holy Spirit comes down. I shall never forget the sound in the district that night—praying in every kraal.

"The next day He came again, and people were on their knees till 6 p.m. This went on for six days and people began to confess their sins and come free as the Holy Spirit brought them through. They had forgiveness of sins, and met the Savior as only the Holy Spirit can reveal Him. Everyone who came near would go under the power of the Spirit. People stood up to give their testimonies, and it was nothing to see twenty-five on their feet at the same time.

"At the end of one week nearly all were through. We had two revival meetings every day for fifteen months without a single break, and meetings all day on Fridays. Hundreds were converted—but we were looking for more—for the ten thousand, upon whom He had told us we had a claim."

As the news reached England of this breaking forth of the Spirit, and its spread to neighboring stations, Mrs. Bessie Porter Head, the wife of Mr. Albert Head, published two booklets. They were called *Advance in Gazaland*, and *Retrospect and Revival in Gazaland*.[1]

Mrs. Head started by giving some account of the founding

---

[1] These extracts are published by kind permission of the South Africa General Mission.

of the Rusitu Station in 1897. Several early pioneers had laid down their lives in founding the work, including Mr. Hatch's first wife. They had been sowing for years, and as Mrs. Head said, after Mr. and Mrs. Howells arrived and the blessing had begun: "The two former [Mr. and Mrs. Hatch] have labored for many years there, truly 'sowing in tears' the seed of life with patience and prayer. The two latter [Mr. and Mrs. Howells] are now helping them to 'reap with joy' a great harvest, which is being gathered in by the power of the Holy Spirit to the glory of God."

After describing the mighty movement of the Spirit on that first Sunday, she continues: "Meetings lasted from early morning till sunset, with only a short interval, the people weeping and confessing their sins, so that the missionaries could not put in a word, but simply wept with them and prayed for them. Sometimes everyone would be kneeling and confessing together in great agony of soul, and then one and another would 'get free' and begin to sing for joy. This went on day by day from Sunday till Thursday, the Spirit doing a mighty convicting work in souls and leading to confessions such as no human agency could have extorted from them . . . .

"Hearing of God's working in such a remarkable manner at Rusitu, an invitation was sent from the American Board Mission Station (some forty miles to the south) to Mr. Hatch and Mr. Howells to visit Mount Silinda. . . . This is a large station with a staff of doctors, minister, school mistresses, etc. . . .

"At the first meeting, at 9 a.m. on Thursday, the building was crowded, and the missionaries told how the blessing had come to Rusitu, and what were the conditions of blessing. After two or three of the Rusitu Christians had given their testimonies, crowds began to cry for mercy, and to confess their sins, the numbers being so great that it was impossible to help them all, though the meeting lasted till one o'clock in the day. All met again at 2 p.m. and there was a wonderful time: the men who had held back somewhat in the morning coming forward in confession of sin, and completely broken down;

teachers, evangelists, and scholars all praying and confessing, and this went on without any confusion under the Spirit's control until sunset. . . .

"As was said previously, none but the Holy Spirit could have made the people confess the sins which burdened them. For instance, a tall man stood up and related in broken voice the following story. In one of the native wars the young men were boasting of how they killed women, etc., so this man went and killed in cold blood a young girl. After he became a Christian, she seemed to be constantly before him, as if asking why he had killed her. As an ordinary Christian, he had thought this was too great a sin to confess, and only Holy Ghost power led to the confession. He wept and wept, and said he was the chief of sinners, and was in agony of soul for hours. But what a scene when he got freed! He could only say, 'Thank you, Lord Jesus.' He began to give his testimony, and said that for years he had not known what peace was, and then he would break out afresh saying, 'Thank you, Lord Jesus!'

"That day about a hundred souls came to complete deliverance and victory, and on Saturday scores came through into the new life of peace and surrender, and instead of soul agony, the majority were praising and singing with joy. On Sunday over two hundred had come into liberty, and there was no need for the missionaries to speak, as four or five were standing at a time each to take their turn to give testimony. . . .

"Perhaps the most blessed outlook for the district is that God mightily met and filled with the Holy Spirit twenty young men and women who some weeks before the revival had offered themselves to the Lord for evangelistic work in Portuguese East Africa. . . .

"As this brief account of God's working goes to the press, further tidings have come to hand of the continued outpouring of God's Spirit in the Gazaland district. . . . During the short visit of Mr. Hatch and Mr. Howells to Melsetter, the power of the Spirit was so mighty in the meetings that white people and black were alike deeply convicted, and lives were wholly surrendered to God. . . . The farmsteads on the road to Melsetter were visited, and six Dutch and English were converted, and four who were already Christians surrendered fully to God . . . .

"Are not these facts encouragements to us all to 'continue instant in prayer,' and will not God continue to show us His 'greater things,' not only in Gazaland, but right throughout South Africa? The little flames that are already alight in different centers may by our prayers be fanned into a mighty blaze . . . ."

Mrs. Howells now continues the story: "At the end of fifteen months, a request came to all the mission stations from the head office of the S.A.G.M. in Cape Town asking the missionaries and Africans to give half an hour every morning from 7 to 7:30 to pray specially that every station might receive the same blessing as we had experienced at Rusitu. Mr. Howells used to go to a little summer-house for this special half-hour of prayer.

"One Monday morning, about a month after starting to pray, I saw Mr. Howells coming in, after he had only been out a quarter of an hour, and I could see by his face that something marvelous had happened to him. He said, 'I was pleading on His word, Malachi 3:10, and I *saw* the Holy Ghost descending. He appeared to me. I *saw* Him coming down on all the mission stations,' and the glory of God was so much on him that he was not in himself. He said he couldn't stay on the station, but must go up to the mountain. He couldn't be still, but for a whole day walked miles upon the mountain shouting praises to God. I followed him until I was too tired for words! He was in that glory all the week — it was so great as to be almost unbearable."

Mr. Howells did not think that he would be the one to go around the stations, until a month later they had an invitation to a Conference at Durban at which all the missionaries who could leave their stations were to be present, and they asked Mr. and Mrs. Howells to bring sufficient clothes for six months as they wanted them to go round the stations. Mr. Howells so shrank from the responsibility of being the one God could use that he said that he couldn't come. "I have only been on the field two years," was his excuse. But the answer came back from Mr. Middlemiss, the Superintendent in Cape Town, "You are a man under authority and you must come!"

Before they left to go down to Durban, Mr. Middlemiss wrote and said, "I know you haven't a banking account [he knew that they had been led to give 50 per cent of their salary away so as to continue to maintain a personal life of faith], so will you wire if you haven't the money for your fare." But Mr. Howells said, "No, I'll never wire. We are going to trust the Lord." He regarded it as a good means of proving that the call was really from the Lord. It came to the last post before they were to leave at 6 a.m. the next day. In that post was a letter from a friend in America, who had never given them money before, sending in dollars the equivalent of £25. So they started their journey in full assurance of faith.

There were forty-three missionaries present at the Conference. Mr. Howells hadn't expected to take part more than anyone else, but the blessing was so great in the opening meetings that he was asked to speak every day. For about three weeks it was like a revival. Some nights the meetings went on into the early hours of the morning, and all the missionaries received a blessing. They were so full of joy that they were even singing on the streetcars.

By the end of the Conference the missionaries gave Mr. Howells a unanimous invitation to visit all the stations, thus confirming the intimation he had already received from the Council at Cape Town. All then went back to their stations to pray and prepare for the visit, in expectation that the Holy Ghost would fall on each station, as He had done at Rusitu.

Mr. Howells continues the story: "How could I believe that there would be scores saved on these stations, where in some cases the ground was still very stony? The enemy challenged me on this and asked me how I could carry revival from one land to another, with different languages, and hundreds of miles between them. I didn't overcome this test in a day. There was many a hard battle, for the issues were tremendous, but I remember when I did come through. I said that there was no need to take people with the blessing from station to station, because the Holy Ghost was going in us, and He is the Author of Pentecost and the Source of revival.

"Our journey took us over 11,000 miles, visiting five countries: Swaziland, Pondoland, Bomvanaland, Tembuland, and Zululand. We were two years away from our own station. On the first station it was hard going the first day. The missionary told us of much backsliding in the church—even some of the deacons had been causing trouble. But on the third day the Spirit came down and swept the place.

"Two of the deacons were always sitting at the back. When the people began to confess their sins and come through to great blessing, they came up to me and said, 'We enjoy the meetings very well, but we don't like this confessing of sins. When it begins, we feel a great pain in the back of our heads!' 'Quite so,' I answered, 'but one day it will move down a little lower—to your hearts!' 'Do you think we need to confess?' they then inquired. 'If you have sinned against God,' I replied, 'it is between you and God; but if you have sinned against the church, you must confess before the church.'

"One of these deacons was named Jephthah. He went to pray and continued in prayer for about three days. Then, about one o'clock in the morning, his wife came and got us up: 'Do come; Jephthah is mad with joy! Shall we ring the bell and call the people together for a meeting?' 'You can't ring the bell at this hour of the night,' I protested. But his mother went round to all the people, calling them together, and by 3 a.m. the church was packed!

"Jephthah was blinded, just like the Apostle Paul. They had to lead him to the church, where he confessed the sins he had been committing. After that, scores were converted. His sight returned in a few days, and we took him around with us for about three months. Whenever he gave his testimony, it was like shots from a gun all the time, as one after another would go down under the Spirit's conviction, and he never failed to get many through.

"In the next place there was a school of ninety-nine girls. They had heard that people were confessing their sins, so they met together and agreed among themselves that they were not going to confess theirs! The first two meetings were very hard in consequence, but at midnight on the second day a cry went up and they could hold out no longer. They began to confess, until ninety-eight were converted; the other one ran away. Many began to pray for their families, who had never been to a meeting.

"The next place we visited was Bethany, where the Queen of Swaziland lived. The first day we were thirteen hours in the chapel, dealing all the time with souls. On the third day, the power that was there! It wasn't the preaching; it was the power! One African prayed, 'Lord, give us a hundred converts in the next three days.' Those were the believings of the Holy Ghost.

"The Queen of Swaziland sent for me. She asked why her people were going after my God. I told her it was because they had met the living God, and had forgiveness of sins and the gift of eternal life. I told her that God had one Son, and He gave Him to die for us; and we had one son and had left him to tell the people of Africa about God. She was very much affected by hearing that my wife and I loved her people more than we loved our own son. She allowed me to have a private meeting with her chief men, but said I must not look at her, but speak as if I were only talking to them! Later in the chapel, the power of God was on the meeting, and when I tested it, fifty stood up, including the young queen, the daughter-in-law of the reigning queen. The man who had prayed for a hundred souls leaped to his feet, exclaiming, 'Praise God for answering prayer. Fifty souls—and the queen, another fifty! We have our hundred!' But before the three days were ended, a hundred and five had accepted Christ!

"When we came back some time later, the old queen asked to see us privately. She told us that she had just lost her daughter, who had also become a Christian, and she had died in perfect peace, trusting in Jesus. She seemed very much affected, and added that she too, in her heart, had accepted the Savior.

"In Pondoland, on one station I was preaching on the crucifixion on Good Friday, and the Spirit brought out those words, 'Away with Him, crucify Him!' It seemed as though the people saw hell opened before them, and in one mass the whole congregation rushed forward to get right with God. I was afraid they would push the pulpit over.

"At another place in Zululand where I was preaching, an evangelist was convicted of lack of power to win souls. He went out to the bush and cried all night to God. The next day he accepted the Holy Spirit. He came through most gloriously, and the outcome of that anointing was such that before very long his out-station had become greater than the main station."

In ways like these the Holy Ghost came down on every station and gave revival, exactly as He had said He would do, and fulfilled the promise of the 10,000 souls. In Johannesburg, for instance, Mr. Howells conducted great revival meetings for twenty-one days in one of the largest churches and it was packed every night. He had to speak through three interpreters, there were so many different tribes, but that did not hinder the Spirit breaking through and hundreds coming out every night for salvation. No one was more conscious than His servant that the Holy Ghost was the Doer of it, and that it was "not by might, nor by power, but by My Spirit." He laid hands on hundreds under the Spirit's power and guidance, and they came free every time. Outside the meetings he would look at his hands, see how ordinary they were, and wonder where the power came from! But he knew!

At the end of the tour, on the way back from Johannesburg to Rusitu, they had been invited by a friend to stay with him in Umtali, which was a railhead. From there they were to get the post-cart which was running to Melsetter, and then finish their journey on horseback or donkey. When they arrived at Umtali their friend met them at the station and told them he was very sorry he could not have them as there was influenza in the house. He suggested their going to the hotel where missionaries usually stayed. They found this would cost them 15s. a day. They had no money, but Mr. Howells said to his wife, "Let's enjoy ourselves; I'm sure the Lord will deliver before the end of the week." So they made a good holiday of it.

The post came by rail on Saturday evening, and they were looking to the Lord to send something by it, as they were leaving next day at 6 a.m. But when they went down to meet the train, they were told there had been a breakdown, and it was not expected that night. "We teased one another that we were not enjoying our meal that evening as much as usual!" said Mr. Howells. "We had told the hotel keeper to have our bill ready for Sunday morning.

"At 5 a.m. he knocked at the door and gave it us. We said we were going up to the post and would pay him at six. At 5:30 a.m. we went, praying all the way. We had a box number in Umtali, to which we had told some of our friends to write.

" 'Is there anything in Box 32?' I asked. The man looked and said, 'Nothing at all, sir.' But in a flash it came to my wife—it was not 32, but 23! There was just one letter. It had five different addresses on it. It had followed us around, and reached us on this very morning with £30 in it!

"As well as the hotel bill, we had to pay £7. 10s. for the post-cart. Although it was hard and springless, it was like the best motorcar to us. We never thought of the cart or the 140 miles—the springs were in us!"

During their first two years Mr. and Mrs. Howells had learned the language Chindau. On their return to Rusitu, they settled in to the normal routine of an African mission station while Mr. and Mrs. Hatch went on furlough. They were left in charge of a boys' and girls' school, as well as the meetings and adults' work. Much must be passed over of their daily experiences during these years; there was, however, one outstanding event.

The revival was still continuing, but there was one special obstacle: hardly any of the married men were converted. They were bound by an age-old custom called Labola, which some think originated with Laban! The fixed price for a wife was £25, which meant a large sum for a father with three or four girls; but a converted man could never sell his daughter, so no married men turned to the Lord. The Spirit then reminded Mr. Howells of his former intercession for a lost soul, and told him to challenge the devil on this point and use the victory of Calvary to set these men free to accept Christ.

He was building a house at the time, so he prayed that he would get married men to work on it. Six of them applied. There were prayers every morning and they were hearing the gospel. The first guidance the Lord gave him was to ask them to come to the Sunday morning service, instead of digging in their gardens. They said they came every morning (but those daily meetings were during their working hours, and they had no objection to being paid for sitting down!). He told them that it would please God much more if they came of their own accord on Sundays. They did come, and five were saved. It was the first break in the enemy's ranks, but there were still hundreds untouched. How could God reach them?

God had a way that was most unexpected. It was the time of the great influenza epidemic which spread over the world just after World War I and caused millions of deaths. Not long after these first five had come through, Mr. Howells heard that the flu had reached their district, and many were down with it. It troubled him that this scourge should come, just when the break among the married men had begun, but the Lord said to him, "Don't you believe Romans 8:28? Can't you trust Me that this is a blessing in disguise?"

The Lord then reminded Mr. Howells of how, in the intercession for sick people in the village at home, he had been led to challenge death a number of times. Would he be able to challenge it again here on a much larger scale? He had already had one very sharp test since coming to Africa, in which he had been able to prove God again for himself in this respect. It had been in an attack of malaria of a very severe form. "I am sure it was allowed just to test this position," he observed, "for when you really face this enemy, you can't make that bold challenge unless you are sure where you stand." After many days of unabated fever, which had resisted all ordinary treatment, Rees was sinking rapidly, and it looked one night as if he would not live till the morning. Mrs. Howells had gone aside for a short time to pray, and while he was alone, the Holy Ghost said to him, "Why don't you ask the Father to heal you?" He thought he had, but the Spirit said to him, "You didn't ask believing." "I just turned over in bed," Mr. Howells said, "and in that moment was healed.

"I wondered if my wife would know it. Would she have lost her burden? She came back to the room, and the moment she opened the door she knew something had happened. 'You have been healed,' she said, and I laughed out loud and told her about it."

Three days later Mr. Howells was out on trek (as they had planned they would be before the fever struck him down), and he was perfectly fit. Although he worked and traveled much in malarious districts after that, it never touched him again.

But this time he was faced with death on a large scale. After their tour of the mission stations, Mr. and Mrs. Howells had been invited by Mr. Charles Murray, the son of Dr. Andrew Murray, to visit his station. But they had just been asked to cancel their visit because of the flu, which had carried away two of the missionaries and scores of the converts.

At Rusitu the flu reached the station first. In four days they had a number down. The heathen said it was a curse from the ancestral spirits, because of the Christians who had broken the Labola. But it soon reached the kraals also, and many were dying.

In two or three days, a deputation came up from the chief and asked, "Have you had any deaths?" "No," replied Mr. Howells. "Have you had any?" "Yes, many," they said. "But can't the witch doctors do anything to help you?" "Oh, two of them were among the first to go down." "But what about your ancestral spirits?" "Our fathers never had this illness," they answered, "so their spirits cannot deal with it." "Quite so," returned Mr. Howells, "the witch doctors have failed and the ancestral spirits have failed—but our God has not failed." "Are none of your people going to die then?" they inquired. The Holy Spirit said to His servant, "Tell them that no one can die on the station." So he answered, "No! Not one will die on the mission station."

"I now had the victory of faith," said Rees Howells, "and the Lord gave guidance about the way to do things. He told me to turn the chapel into a hospital, and to put fires in at night, so that the temperature was kept even. If I had not had those fifteen months of medical training I should have been at sea, but there was no need to make a mistake. The number of cases increased till about fifty were down at a time.

"A few days later a second deputation arrived. 'Have you had any deaths yet?' was their first question. 'Not one,' I told them. 'Are you going to have any?' 'No. Not one will die on the mission station.' Would I have said that unless I knew that the Holy Ghost was stronger than death? 'Well,' they said, 'the chief has sent us to ask whether, if this disease comes, some of us can come to the mission station to escape death.' 'Tell the chief,' I said, 'that any of your people that want can come to the station. We will look after them, and not one will die. But remember this—if you come, you must admit that our God is the living God, and that He can help where the witch doctors and the ancestral spirits have failed!'"

A few hours later, he saw a mournful procession wending its way toward the station—five of the worst, gospel-hardened sinners among the married men! Slowly they came with blankets over their heads and the fear of death on their faces—their wives in the rear, carrying their sleeping mats and drinking cups. "How I praised God for my personal Guide!" Mr. Howells said.

After that dozens of them came up. Mr. Howells worked day and night on the people for three months. Mrs. Howells labored with him, until she herself succumbed to it. She was desperately ill for eight days, but one thing Mr. Howells told her—she could not die!

At one point he felt that he was touched with it himself, fatigued as he was through lack of sleep and the prolonged trial. But just as he was attending to one of the patients, the Lord spoke to him: "If I can keep death from the station, and you are needed to look after these sick ones, don't you believe that I can keep the germ from overcoming you?" His faith took hold of it, and he said, "I had the victory that moment. It was then I learned that hymn, 'In God I have found a retreat,' where the last verse says:

> *A thousand may fall at my side,*
> *And ten thousand at my right hand,*
> *Above me His wings are spread wide,*
> *Beneath them in safety I stand.*

I found the Holy Spirit in me was stronger than the flu. What it was to live with God in a plague!

"I had two cases which tested me very much," he added. "If the devil could take them, he could take about fifty. I did everything medically for them, but I couldn't move the temperature, no matter what I tried. So I brought them before the Lord, and pleaded His Word. The moment I got victory, their temperatures dropped and they were safe. There was not a single death."

Through a region of about twenty miles' radius the news spread that the God of the white man was stronger than death. Conviction of sin took hold of many, and of those who came to the station, many found the Savior. The greatness of the Lord's victory was seen in the fact that after this epidemic was over, in the meetings the whole of one side of the chapel was filled with married men. Mr. Howells said, "I told the Holy Spirit, 'How wonderful You are! You have preached more to the Africans in this way than through any of my words!' "

After the revival, some of their men who were full of the Holy Ghost used to go down on trek into Portuguese East Africa, between the mission station and the port of Beira. Some of the people there received blessing, and those who were converted built a little place of worship, although they had been warned by the Roman Catholics that they must not pray together. One Sunday morning six soldiers marched into the little chapel and took thirty-two of them prisoners, and kept them—men, women, and children—in prison for four months. But not one of the prisoners would give in; 'they had the spirit of the martyrs.' After four months, they released the women and children, but forced them to drink beer. To the six men they said that if they would stop preaching, they also could go out that day. They refused, saying that if they were released, they would preach the next day. They were kept in prison for two years, and four of them died there.

They were questioned and persecuted all the time, because their jailors couldn't understand what it was they had. Their shouts of praise and joy used to annoy them, so they separated Matthew, their leader, and put him in with an old heathen man, a greater sinner, who was always in prison. They heard nothing the first or second night, and were delighted that they had stopped the shouting. But the next night it was worse than ever—not only Matthew rejoicing, but the old heathen man shouting praises to God because he had been saved!

Matthew caught smallpox in prison. He knew he was going to die, so he called all his friends together and told them he was going to be with the Lord, and that they must stand fast in the faith; then he bade farewell to them, and went home to glory.

Mr. Howells concluded that the only way to get a permanent footing in that country would be to buy a farm, which was offered them by a Frenchman, costing £1,200. When Timothy, their head teacher at Rusitu, and the others heard of it, they said, "We will all give a third of our salary to help buy it." The Howells were so touched by their example that they felt, in addition to the 50 per cent of their salary they were already giving, they should give a further thank-offering of £100.

Soon after this, when they were on furlough, Mr. Howells was telling in a Convention about Matthew and what had happened in Portuguese East Africa. He didn't say a word about money, but he hadn't been speaking five minutes before a woman in the hall stood up and said, "I'll pay for that farm."

The Lord told Mr. Howells not to take all that money, because she was under the influence of the meeting, so he said to her afterwards, "I don't expect you to give more than I give— £100." Her brother then said he would give £100, and two other people came and said they would give £100 each. He went to Birmingham and again had a gift of £100. He went to Dundee, and one morning under his plate found £100. Again in Glasgow another man said, "If Matthew gave his blood, I'll give you £100." Altogether he had £1,100 in £100 gifts. In the end that actual farm was not bought, but several centers were opened in the territory.

So ended their period in Africa. "It was perfect victory," said Mr. Howells. "I don't think we had anything to cause us an hour's trouble, and for both my wife and myself, they were the six happiest years of our lives."

25

Buying the First Estate in Wales

Mr. and Mrs. Howells arrived home at Christmas, 1920. At the mission headquarters people said they had never seen a couple come on furlough looking so well. "We've been having six years' vacation," said Mr. Howells, and wanted to start meetings at once!

The Council insisted on at least a few weeks' rest, but they found even six weeks hard to bear. When the start was made, it was non-stop for three years. Mr. Howells' testimony of revival created a great stir. Doors opened to him everywhere and there was tremendous blessing; in fact, to hundreds who heard him, it was something unique. The Council of the Mission recognized the Spirit's working as so unusual that they made him a free lance and asked him to spend five years traveling all over the English-speaking world as God might lead him and taking his testimony to God's people everywhere.

It was the very thing Rees Howells most wanted to do. "I couldn't think of any position to compare with that," he said, "preaching to tens of thousands of people, and the Lord blessing. Before I was converted, I had it in me to travel the world, and gave that up, and here the Lord was giving it back."

But, once again, the entirely unexpected was to happen. While he was preaching to the large audience at the Llandrindod Convention of 1922, the power was so great that, although he was the first speaker at one meeting, the chairman, Mr. Head, asked him to make an appeal for full surrender. The whole audience—chairman, speakers, and congregation, rose to their feet. The speaker who was to follow, Rev. G. H. Lunn, said that it would be quite out of place for him to give his address, and the meeting closed.

Immediately afterwards, a minister asked Mr. Howells and several others to join him for prayer. He put before them the fact of so many young people responding to God's call and the urgent need of more training facilities in Wales, and he suggested that they ask the Lord for a training college. It never dawned on Mr. Howells that he was to have a part in it. But as they got down to pray, the Lord said to him, "Be careful how you pray. I am going to build a college, and build it through you!"

It came as such a shock to him that the only thing he could say was, "If You are really speaking to me, confirm it through the Word," and that night the confirmation came to him through 1 Chronicles 28:20,21, where these three promises stood out before him, "Be strong . . . and do it . . . for the Lord God will be with thee; He will not fail thee, nor forsake thee, until thou hast finished all the work . . . of the house of the Lord"; "There shall be with thee . . . every willing, skillful man, for any manner of service"; and the third from the next chapter (29:4), that the Lord would give him a talent of gold, which from the margin of his Scofield Bible he learned was worth £6,150.

As he and his wife prayed this over, it came as a great test. It meant being called away from the very thing that most appealed to them—a world-wide revival ministry. It also meant new and large financial burdens, for the Lord told them that they would have to do it by faith, whereas in their present work all finances were provided. And worst of all, having left one son to go to Africa, it would now mean leaving hundreds of spiritual children in Africa.

They were preparing to go to America on a private visit, leaving in three days' time, so they took a bold step. They asked the Lord to seal the new call by sending the very next day the money they would need for the whole trip. It was not an easy request, because there was no reason why people should give them money, knowing they were receiving allowances as missionaries. But the next day the Lord gave them personal gifts amounting to £138, including £50 from a man who had been blessed through Mr. Howells eleven years before, and had told the Lord that if he ever met him again he would give him that sum. The gifts seemed so sacred to them that they gave £100 as a thank-offering to the Mission, just as David poured out the water from the well of Bethlehem before the Lord.

While in America they spoke to many congregations and visited well-known centers, such as the Fulton Street Prayer Meeting in New York. But one place, the Moody Bible Institute in Chicago, impressed Mr. Howells more than any other. "It was worth going 4,000 miles if only to see that Institute," he said. "Of all the sights, that was the greatest. Nine hundred men and women hand-picked by God."

And it was while he was sitting on the platform before speaking that the Lord finally settled the matter of the college for him. He asked him, "Can I build a college like this in Wales?" "Yes, You can," he answered; "You are God." "But what I am to do, I am to do through man. You are going to tell these young people that I came to dwell in you. Can I build that college through *you*?" "I believed God that second," said Mr. Howells. "The College was built that second!"

On their return home to Brynamman, together they made a final dedication of themselves to the new call. They went up their favorite Black Mountain, and kneeling there, gave themselves over to the Lord to be His instruments to raise up a college. All the money they had between them that day was 16s.!

One sad consequence was that it meant resigning from the Mission, which was a great wrench on both sides. The Council did not want to let them go, and they would not have left the Mission and the co-workers they had learned to love for anything less than a direct command from God.

They had no idea where the College was to be. Like Abraham, they went out not knowing whither they went. In the early summer of that year, 1923, a friend offered them his furnished house for a vacation in a seaside town. They went there expecting to enjoy it, but as soon as they arrived, a curious thing happened. Mr. Howells felt strongly that they should not be there. "I don't know that I ever disliked a place before," he said, "but I told my wife, 'I don't like it here. Let's go to the place my father spoke about—to Mumbles.' I laughed at this, getting a home for nothing and then not wanting it. But the moment we went to Mumbles, I knew it was the place where God wanted us to be." They were in lodgings there for a month, and Mr. Howells spent his time on the cliffs, not to enjoy the sea but to be alone with God, wondering what the next step was to be.

One morning two of his friends, Professor Keri Evans and the Rev. W.W. Lewis, met with him for prayer. Hearing that he did not yet know where the College was to be, Mr. Keri Evans suggested Swansea. Wondering if that could be of the Lord, Mr. Howells made a definite request in prayer: "If Swansea is the place, show me the College before I go to Keswick next week." The answer came back: "I will show you tomorrow."

The next day, as Mr. and Mrs. Howells were walking along the Mumbles Road, which skirts Swansea Bay, they passed a large estate on the rising ground overlooking the bay, and noticed that the house was vacant. They went up to the gate, and found the name of the place to be Glynderwen, and as they stood there, the Lord's word came: "This is the College!"

Mr. Howells continues the story in his own words: "What a mansion it looked to me! I had no idea of the value of such a place, but I supposed it would be worth £10,000; and all the money we had between us was two shillings! I remember the impression it made on me—buying a place like that by faith!

"The gardener informed us that Mr. William Edwards, J.P., the draper, was the owner. The Spirit then told me to ask the Lord for a confirmation in the impossible, as a proof that He had spoken, for when God gives a proof like that, you can be sure that it is He and not man. So I asked Him to send to me within two days a man who knew the owner—and we didn't know *anyone* in Mumbles!

"What were my feelings the next day? Very mixed, because I knew what it would mean to build a college. If I didn't get the proof, then I would be free, and could again enjoy the liberty I had had during the past ten years. On the other hand, if the proof came, I would have to commit myself and take up the fight.

"About ten o'clock the following morning, the local minister called. We had attended his chapel the previous Sunday, when he was away, and hearing we were missionaries, he had come to ask us to tea. 'Do you know Mr. Edwards, the draper?' I inquired. 'Yes,' he said, 'very well.' That was God! But in a moment a dark cloud came over me, and I knew that I should never be free again until that college was built. Only those who have gone the same way can understand what that meant.

"I called to see Mr. Edwards, but I felt as weak as a man recovering from fever. Oh the burden, the heaviness, the very powers of hell seemed against me! The devil said I was always doing things my own way, with no money and no business training. It seemed as if I hadn't strength to ring the bell. When I told him why I had come, he said, 'Other religious people are after the place, but not the same religion as yours. I am going to London today. If you come and see me again, I will consider it.' But he obviously thought a missionary couldn't buy such a building! For one thing, he said there was a tavern on the estate, and what would I want with a place like that? What moments they were when I left him! Had I done wrong?

"I went to see the property again next day, and while talking to the gardener, he remarked, 'The Catholics have bought this house.' 'Never!' I said. Then the Lord told me, 'That's why I called you to buy this place. I brought you back from Africa to make a test case for Me with the Church of Rome.' They had been responsible for the death of six of our best men in Portuguese East Africa; that was my only touch with them, and everything in me was roused against them. I knew they were buying places near every university, and no one was stopping them. I realized the Holy Spirit was now saying He would never have allowed the Church of Rome to have power again in this country if He had found men to believe Him; and His word to me was plain: 'I shall be very displeased with you if they get this property.'

"In a moment I saw it was a contest with the wealthiest church in the world, and I said, 'But You haven't given me money.' 'Didn't I promise you a talent of gold?' He replied. 'If you believe, go on your knees here and claim this place.' So I knelt down there on the lawn by the little bridge and claimed it, and declared aloud, 'They will never get this property. I take it for the Lord.' "

A few days later Rees Howells spoke to Mr. Edwards again, who asked him a direct question. "If I put these other people off, will you 'close' with me on it?" Mr. Howells knew so little about buying properties that he first had to inquire what that expression meant! He then promised to do so in two weeks, after his return from the Keswick Convention.

While in Keswick, God gave him another marvelous confirmation. An invitation came to preach in Anwoth parish, in southern Scotland. Faced with such a big decision in Swansea they would not have gone but for the definite guidance of the Spirit. But as soon as they arrived in Anwoth, the lady with whom they stayed, Mrs. Stewart, the widow of the former Consul-General in Persia, told them that in front of their bedroom window scores of the Covenanters had been martyred. "That's God," said Mr. Howells, "the guidance is right again, taking us up here against ourselves, as it were."

The following day they were invited to tea with Sir William and Lady Maxwell, at Cardoness House. The first thing he did was to take them to a small room where a framed document hung on the wall. "I am going to show you the most precious deed in Scotland," he said, "—the deed signed by the blood of the Covenanters."

"When he said that," continued Mr. Howells, "I felt my blood run cold. To think that in Glynderwen the Lord had told me He had brought me back to make a test case with the Church of Rome, and here I was face to face with the

Covenanters' deed. It is a wonder I remained standing on my feet. There were the signatures scrawled in blood as if with bits of stick. When I saw it, I changed altogether, and there wasn't one thing I wouldn't do to vindicate the Holy Spirit.

"I never felt anything like it before or since. I shed tears that night in my room. I said to the Holy Ghost, 'If it costs my blood, I'll do this for You. If Mr. Edwards asks for £10,000, I'll pay it, and if the Church of Rome puts a match to Glynderwen the next day and burns it to ashes, I'll say it is the best investment I ever made.'

"The Spirit of God came on me to fight that church: it was God's anger in me towards the Church of Rome, keeping those five hundred million souls in darkness on the Continent and elsewhere. I entered into a world where fellowship with people was not to count; the only fellowship was with those martyrs who had laid down their lives for the liberty of the gospel. When I saw that deed, the strength of God came into me and changed my body from clay to steel!"[1]

---

[1]Concerning this deed, Mr. J. Purves, who is the author of *Sweet Believing*, a book on the Covenanters, has kindly sent us the following note:

"Through the Royal Stuarts, their Divine Right of Kings, and their laws and aims in the State Church, the power of Rome overshadowed Scotland almost all of the seventeenth century. At the end of February 1638 the National Covenant was drawn up by spiritual leaders of the land and eagerly subscribed to by many thousands, saying, 'In special we detest and refuse the usurped authority of that Roman Antichrist upon the Scriptures of God, upon the kirk, the civil magistrate and conscience of men,' and accordingly setting forth a clear and literal restatement of the Reformed Faith as given in the Confession of faith of 1580-81. It was the open protest of a nation against Popery, and a reasserting of the Scriptural views of the Gospel of Salvation. It solemnly pledged all who signed it to promote evangelical doctrine and discipline in all their Scriptural purity.

"Preserved in the Museum of the Corporation of Edinburgh is the great original, a parchment of deerskin with 3,250 names and initials on it, some evidently written in blood. It was subscribed in Greyfriars Churchyard, Edinburgh, February 28, 1638. Copies of this

When Mr. Howells returned from Keswick, Mr. Edwards made him a definite offer of Glynderwen for £6,300. "I thought he would have asked more than that," said Mr. Howells, "and meant to accept his offer; but the Lord said, 'No! It was a talent of gold I promised you—£6,150, and not a penny more.' I stood against God in a second; I showed my attitude towards Him, but He didn't say another word and I knew I wouldn't dare disobey Him.

"When I questioned his price, Mr. Edwards told me to discuss the matter with his solicitor the next day. But instead, I went to a friend's house in Llanelly, where for two days I neither ate nor drank. What agony I went through, but what lessons I learned!

"I told God that He had called me to fight the Church of Rome, and here He was quibbling over £150; but He turned it back on me. Hadn't I claimed Glynderwen for Him? Didn't I believe, then, that the Catholics wouldn't get it? If the battle had been won in Scotland, could the Holy Ghost ever allow Mr. Edwards to sell the property to anyone else?

"I was beginning to get strong now. Was Mr. Edwards in the hands of the Holy Ghost? Could the devil induce him to sell it? During the two days I came right through, and what

National Covenant were immediately sent all over the country, even to as far away as London, for signatures. At present there are nearly fifty copies known and preserved. It was one of them, greatly treasured, that Mr. Rees Howells saw at Cardoness House, signed by some of those who suffered unto death. Copies prepared for signatures were usually written on large sheets of vellum. The one at Cardoness House is the only printed copy whose existence is known of that great document, which when read in the churches of 1638 'was heartily embraced, sworn and subscribed with tears and great joy.'

"I am indebted to Colonel F. Rainsford-Hannay of Cardoness House for so kindly furnishing details showing the authenticity of the Cardoness copy of the National Covenant on which the honoured names of peer and commoner are set side by side. Mrs. Rainsford-Hannay is a daughter of the late Sir William and Lady Maxwell who entertained Mr. Rees Howells at Cardoness House."

liberty I had! Whatever price the enemy offered, he could never get it. I had heard that Mr. Edwards was a great businessman, but I had to learn that God could control him. I came to the place where I knew that whenever God wants to take over a property, the owner has very little to do with it!

"When I returned home I received a letter from Mr. Edwards saying that all negotiations were off. As I had not gone to the solicitor, I had proved that I was not a businessman, and he would sell to the other people, who were offering him £10,000.

"I was not affected by the letter, because the Unseen Captain had taken over, and the responsibility was not mine any longer. I wrote Mr. Edwards and told him quite plainly that it was much harder for me to refuse his offer of £6,300 than to accept it; but God had said I was not to go above £6,150, and after spending two days with Him neither eating nor drinking, He had confirmed His word to me. I had a letter by return, saying he would drop the price £500! He refused to make a single penny on it. Wasn't that God?"

When the agreement had been signed, Mr. Howells had ten days in which to pay the deposit. On the day he was due to go to the solicitor with the money, he was £140 short. He was still short this sum when the actual hour arrived, so in faith he set off to the office without it. He hadn't been there long when Mrs. Howells arrived. She had followed him down with the post, and in it were three checks, which made up the £140 to the penny!

But the real battle came over the full sum to be paid. He had never dealt in large amounts before, and the burden was great upon him. He was to take no meetings, nor make any appeals. His eyes were to be on God alone. He gave himself to prayer, spending his days in his little upstairs bedroom in his mother's home, alone with God and His Word from 6 a.m. to 5 p.m., when he took his first meal. In the evenings he continued in prayer with his newly found prayer-partner, Mr. Tommy Howells. Ten months were spent in this way until the victory was complete.

It was during this time that God established for him the principles of faith in finance which were to govern all his future large-scale dealings in the purchase of properties, and their upkeep. At that time, George Muller was the only man he knew of who had done the same thing before—with no council, no denomination, not making his needs known, and shut in with God alone. Mr. Howells found him a very great help in proving that the promises of God were reliable to step out on. Indeed he said that the only two books which he found could help him through this critical period were the Bible and Muller's autobiography. He was often encouraged by thinking, "It must be true, because Muller did it." He was determined not to go beyond what Muller did, which was not to buy or build until he had three-quarters of the money.

But in his daily pleadings with the Lord for the promised talent of gold, the Spirit reminded him of something else—the book of Haggai. When the Jews had begun to build the second temple, and the work had stopped through the accusations of their enemies, the Lord through Haggai told them to go on and build, though they were in great poverty. It was then God said to them: "The silver is Mine and the gold is Mine" (Hag. 2:8). When they began to build on the strength of that promise, in faraway Babylon God stirred King Darius to look up the records of what Cyrus had promised them, and to send them all they needed (Ezra 6).

After facing Rees Howells with this passage, the Lord said, "If you believe I am the owner of the silver and gold, as you build I will give you whatever is needed." In other words, the Lord was leading His servant differently from Muller. He was not to wait until he had three-quarters of the money, but he was to go straight ahead and not expect a deliverance from God today for a need of tomorrow. The Lord had taught him years before in small things that "the promises of God are equal to current coin" and that, therefore, he must act on the promises as he would if he actually had the cash.

But he never thought he would be called to apply it on this large scale! It meant many severe tests, and he did not hesitate to use normal business methods of advances from the bank when guided to do so. But the proof that God has been with His servant in this way as He was with George Muller in another is that there are no debts or mortgages today on estates whose present value is about £100,000.

But to return to the purchase of Glynderwen. The next sum asked for was £2,000. The Lord sent gifts varying from 5s. to £300 during the next three months, but when he still only had £1,700, the solicitor suddenly called for it to be paid by eleven o'clock the next morning. At first he was baffled a bit, as to why the Lord had allowed this sudden demand to be made. He was walking down Wind Street in Swansea, and as he came under the bridge the word came to him, "Trust ye in the Lord for ever, for in the Lord Jehovah are everlasting resources." It was a word from heaven to him, and he believed that by eleven o'clock the next morning he would be passing back under that bridge having the money with him. Rees had a train to catch, and finding an empty carriage, he got down on his knees and praised the Lord. He could have danced for joy!

The next morning he had the £300! The woman who sent it told him afterwards that she had a great burden for him during the very same half-hour that he believed. It was so heavy on her that she had to close her shop and post the money off to him. He was able to pay the £2,000 that day with £18 left!

Glynderwen had been the home of Sir Charles Eden, an uncle of the Right Honorable Anthony Eden. The estate consisted of a mansion and eight acres of land, also the tavern. The property had been laid out in lawns, gardens and a tennis court with a lovely view of Swansea Bay and Mumbles.

During the testing days, before the £2,000 was paid, an offer came to buy from Mr. Howells the tavern and four acres of land attached to it. No new liquor license had been granted in Swansea for many years, so the license alone was worth over £1,000, and acceptance would have supplied the extra money needed at that time. It was the first serious temptation in finance to take an easy way of deliverance.

But there was no possibility of compromise on principle.

The offer was turned down, the tavern closed, and the value of the pub license forfeited. Also, the licensee was compensated for clearing out. Fair is fair to all—saints and publicans alike! Then by the addition of eight rooms, the pub itself was converted into a men's dormitory.

The whole property was placed in the hands of three trustees, who stood together in this venture of faith: they were the late Rev. W. W. Lewis, a well-known and respected minister in Swansea; Mr. Henry Griffiths, who was then the confidential clerk of the Great Mountain Colliery Company, and later a Group Accountant of the National Coal Board; and the third was Rees Howells.

Mr. Edwards, the former owner, became very friendly with Mr. Howells, and in later years gave gifts to the work. He confided, "I couldn't sell the property to anyone else." When the completed account was received, with about twenty items on it (including the solicitor's charges and the sum paid to the licensee of the tavern), the total came to £6,150 7s. 4d.—a talent of gold plus 7s. 4d!

The opening of the College was on Whitmonday, 1924, and crowds came to hear the story of what God had done during that great period of commercial embarrassment and scarcity of money. About a thousand people gathered.

"I remember how God tested me," recalled Mr. Howells. "We hadn't a tent or a building then sufficient to hold a crowd, and the meetings would have to be in the open air. It had been raining nearly all the week before. I had ordered hundreds of chairs from the Corporation. On Sunday I had the victory that the Whitmonday would be fine. It was a perfect day. I told the people there would not be a drop of rain till they arrived home that day."

One of the future tutors of the College, a Greek and Hebrew scholar, the Rev. Llynfi Davies, M.A., B.D., testified later how he had come down to that meeting a modernist and went back a believer!

Failing to find any committee or religious body behind it, the press called it "God's College"—an appropriate title!

26

The Bible College of Wales

For the first twelve months after the opening of the College everything was a great success. There were five tutors and thirty-eight students. News of the College was in all the South Wales papers, and at the end of the first session a Convention was held which was attended by about forty ministers. But no work of God can become established unless it goes through the fire. Just because of its rising popularity God had to take the College into death so that it should have none to trust in except Himself, just as years before He had taken His servant personally from popularity and the public eye into the hidden walk which few understood.

During the summer vacation the Lord had been showing Mr. Howells that He was not entirely satisfied with the College. There was worldliness among the students and unwillingness for the standards of faith and surrender which the Holy Spirit had said were to be presented and maintained in the College. The Lord warned him that trouble was coming, but that through it He would purge the work, to His own glory. Even so, it was not realized quite how severe the test would be.

Shortly after the opening of the second session there arose a sharp internal conflict, which ultimately reduced the personnel to a staff of two with five students. There would be no profit now, after all these years, in attempting to go into details. Wounds in the body of Christ are always grievous and put us in the dust at the feet of Him who died to make us one. Yet

God has wonderful ways of bringing good out of evil, and He did just that for the College.

So far as Mr. Howells himself was concerned, God gave him one definite word: "Where there is no tale-bearer, the strife ceaseth." Therefore he would not allow a word to be spoken to him against those who had left. The Lord recalled the position He had brought him to of being able to love the missionary in Madeira and, without needing weeks to "come up to it" this time, he found he was able to pray for God's blessing as much on those who had left as on those who had remained.

For twelve months they didn't have a single lecture, and many thought the College would never rise again. But the time was spent shut in with God in prayer, and they were able to prove that the work did not depend on human support or popularity. "Through this experience," said Mr. Howells, "the College was put on the Rock of Ages: on a foundation that no man nor devil could ever shake." Remarkably enough, they had seldom had big gifts up till then, but from that time onwards God began to send in large sums of money.

Five years later, for the fifth anniversary, on Whitmonday, 1929, Mr. Howells published the first printed report. In it he said:

> We want to give you a brief account of what has been accomplished during the last five years through faith and believing prayer. Thousands were watching the outcome of this venture of faith—a college without a committee, council, denomination, or a wealthy person behind it. No appeal was to be made for finance; one of the chief aims was to strengthen the faith of God's people by giving a visible proof that He is the living and faithful God. . . . The needs of the College as it stands today run up to nearly £5 a day (nearly £35 a week).
>
> During the last three years it has been a rare case to have means in hand to meet our necessities for three days together. It has been the Father's will to teach us the way to trust Him each morning for the day's need, to give a practical demonstration of the words: Give us this day our daily bread. These years have been a time of great financial embarrassment in the world; scar-

city of money and financial pressure have made men's hearts fail them, and many have not been able to stand the strain: but the Lord has been proving us day by day, that living faith is above circumstances; no delays can discourage it, no loss of friends nor depression in trade can touch it.

During this period the Lord has allowed us to be tested beyond our strength; often "pressed out of measure, above strength . . . that we should not trust in ourselves." Our faith has grown with the work, and we have proved over and over again that all the testings have been for the purpose of strengthening it. If we were able a few years ago to take the challenge to build a college when we only had two shillings, and by now have received £8,000, without a single appeal, this in itself is a great encouragement to trust still more.

We have six tutors on our staff, four of them having taken their degrees in different universities of our country; the other two are outstanding ministers in the town. We have thirty students in the College, men and women, who have been called by the Holy Ghost, and have gladly entered the school of faith. Tuition is given free, and the board and residence made as low as possible. Through the gifts sent in to the College in answer to believing prayer, we have been able to give it for nearly half the actual cost.

27

Buying the Second Estate

For two years the Lord had been burdening Rees Howells with the need of taking another property, to provide accomodation for double the number of students. The word he had received was: "Enlarge the place of thy tent, stretch forth the curtains of thine habitation, lengthen thy cords."

A month before the printing of that first report, Mr. Howells heard of the death of Sir Charles Ruthen, the owner of Derwen Fawr, a beautiful estate just up the road from Glynderwen. ("Derwen Fawr" is Welsh for "Great Oak." The ancient tree still stands on the grounds.) Sir Charles had been Director of Housing for the Ministry of Health, and had spent thousands of pounds on the property, buying up all the land between it and the Mumbles Road to prevent anything from blocking the view of Swansea Bay. It consisted of a large house, three cottages, and seventeen acres of grounds.

Sir Charles had dispayed his skill as an architect in altering the house, in laying out acres of lands in lawns and flower beds, and in making the beautiful Italian gardens, for which he had costly stonework brought from Italy, involving a total outlay of over £20,000. Among guests who had stayed there had been Mr. Lloyd George and his family when he was Prime Minister, Lord Melchett, and other Cabinet Ministers. The land was increasing in value, for the town of Swansea had been steadily moving in the Mumbles direction, and Derwen Fawr is the nearest large estate to the University College.

The Lord then revealed to Mr. Howells that Derwen Fawr was the next property he was to buy, so he began to put prayer around it and sometimes to walk with his friends around the wall of the estate as round the walls of Jericho. Not long after, he heard that Lady Ruthen had put it up for sale, and once again that the Church of Rome was bidding for it. In face of such a test, Mr. Howells felt the need of a sign from God. He felt the seriousness of the position for, if they could acquire this property, they could establish a center close to the University. He was sure that God was again calling him to "go against that enemy in the Church of Rome," so he asked Him to confirm it by sending him a big check the very next day from a source from which he had never had money before. On the morrow the first post came with no money; the second with none; but in the third was a letter with £100 from someone who had never given before!

Just at that time the great financial depression was at its worst, and Britain had to go off the gold standard. It was the worst possible time to undertake another great liability but the burden on him was heavy. "The Lord always shows you all the difficulties," he said, "when He is going to do anything through you." So he felt led to ask yet one other sign. His fiftieth birthday was in a few days, and he asked the Lord to send him a check of £50, a pound for each year, and that again it might come from a new source. "I can remember now the meeting we had the night before," he said, "praising before the victory! We were in the run of believing great things." The morning came and all the staff and students were watching for the deliverance. Strangely, the postman only brought one letter, from Scotland. "With excitement we opened it, to find therein a check of £50 from an entirely new donor."

He took the gift to his cousin, Dr. John Howells, who had a practice in Swansea, and showed it to him as the sign that he was to be the owner of Derwen Fawr. The doctor got in touch with Lady Ruthen, and a few days later the two of them went to see the estate and she gave Mr. Howells a promise of the first refusal.

The remarkable thing was that on the very same day that they made this first visit to Lady Ruthen, they met the agent for the Roman Catholics, who had been sent down from London to look over the property! "But the Lord arranged the weather," said Mr. Howells. "It was a dismal day, wet and misty, so that I am sure he did not see over half the place. The grounds had become overgrown, and he must have gone away with a very poor impression."

But Mr. Howells was "face to face with the enemy." His test had come. Would he make the first offer? They had offered £4,000 more for Glynderwen than he gave for it; what would they offer for Derwen Fawr? He went up to the agent and gave his figure. The agent was favorable, and asked him to call again after the weekend.

"I remember the thought of what I had done coming over me," said Mr. Howells. "I still had a liability for Glynderwen, and here I was taking on about £10,000 again. I was away preaching that Sunday. When I went to bed on Saturday night I could not sleep, so I got out of bed and went downstairs to fight it out. It meant a sudden plunge of thousands of pounds without a penny in hand. Only those who have put their hand to the plough and cannot look back can know what it meant.

"All the fasting in the world is nothing to be compared with carrying liability. I would never have done it for my own family, but only for the Kingdom. The devil told me plainly that if I bought Derwen Fawr on top of Glynderwen, I should be in the bankruptcy court. I saw myself there. But when he named the word 'bankrupt,' I also told him, 'When I was in Scotland, I said if I were to pay £10,000 for Glynderwen and the Catholics were to burn it to ashes the next day, it would still be the best investment I had ever made. So I am not only willing to be bankrupt for Derwen Fawr, but I am willing to give the last drop of my blood to save it from the Church of Rome.' The moment I said it, I came through. I felt as free as a bird in my preaching on Sunday.

"On Monday morning I came back to Swansea and went to the agent to learn whether the negotiations had been successful.

He had not come in, and while walking in the town waiting for him I met a friend who asked me where I had been over the weekend. He said he had not been able to get me out of his mind. 'No wonder!' I said, 'I have been in the bankruptcy court!' and I described the victory of Saturday night.

"He stood for a while in thought, and then said, 'Why are you left to fight this battle alone? Are you the only Protestant in the world?' 'It looks like it,' I said. 'Well, you are not to stand alone in this,' he went on. 'If the Covenanters gave their blood to win this liberty for us, I too will give something to maintain it. Go to your agent, and if your offer is accepted come back to me for the deposit.' Victory beyond value!

"We both stood still with tears of joy in our eyes. It had been a stiff climb, but I was able to say with Abraham, 'Jehovah-Jireh—in the mount of the Lord it shall be seen.' And I, too, seemed to hear those words God spoke to His servant: 'Because thou hast done this thing . . . in blessing I will bless thee . . . because thou hast obeyed My voice.' Deliverance is always found on 'the mount'; living faith must first prove to God that it has taken His word and promise for victory."

When the agent arrived, he said there would be some delay in the negotiations. The Lord then told Mr. Howells to make the challenge known. So he sent out 4,000 booklets telling of the Lord's guidance, and saying, "The negotiations are going on, and now that the Lord has given the victory in faith, we believe 'Jehovah-Jireh' will very soon be written over that wonderful property."

A few weeks later the Catholics dropped out of the running, possibly owing to the unfavorable report of their agent. But there was also another syndicate after the property, for local contractors knew it was one of the most desirable building estates in Swansea, and through weeks of tension it was touch and go between them and the College.

The only claim Mr. Howells had was the promise of the first refusal Lady Ruthen had given him. He went to the solicitor's office one Saturday to make a final settlement, but the solicitor said he was busy and told Mr. Howells to return on

Monday. He could see the solicitor was putting him off, so on the Monday he asked his cousin, the doctor, to accompany him.

"It was a day of climax we shall long remember," recalled Mr. Howells. "Only the clerk was in the office when we arrived. She said the solicitor was at his home ill, but he had sent a message for me saying that Derwen Fawr was sold! This was too much for my cousin, and he did not mince matters in what he said. Now indeed was the prediction sorely tested. Was it really from God or from man? If it was from God, Derwen Fawr could never be sold to another person.

"As we left the office, the Lord gave me strength to say to my cousin, 'Derwen Fawr is *not* sold.' His reply was with plenty of emphasis: 'Didn't you hear the girl say Derwen Fawr *is* sold? How can you say it isn't?' 'Because the Lord told me to buy it,' I answered. 'Months ago I put it in print.' Then I said to him, 'Will you go down to the solicitor [an old patient of my cousin's] and see him?' He agreed to do this and set off immediately.

"The daughter answered the door. No one, she said, could visit her father; he was too ill to see any visitors. 'It's the first time I ever heard that a patient was too ill to see a doctor,' my cousin answered, and walked right in. There he learned that the Syndicate had actually sent a check for the deposit to the solicitor's office, which would have been accepted that morning if he had not been ill. But at that 'eleventh hour' he agreed to turn them down.

"The Lord then said to me, 'You must buy Derwen Fawr tonight or never.' So that night my wife and I went up to see Lady Ruthen. As we walked up the drive we saw all the lights being turned out! 'Look,' the enemy said, 'they know you are coming, and don't want to see you!'

Lady Ruthen was wavering, and said she was seriously considering retaining the house for herself. But I reminded her of her promise, and her son-in-law confirmed it. I then offered £500 more than the Syndicate and it was settled. Her son-in-law asked me to give the solicitor some token payment until the proper contract could be signed. All I had in the world was £25, from two gifts I had received that day, so that was my first deposit!''

The decision to buy had been made on Christmas Eve, at the price of £8,000. Within three days Mr. Howells received five gifts of £250, £300, £50, £25, and £50 which, with some other smaller sums, enabled him to pay the legal deposit and secure the property. He was not led to accept the kind offer made a few months before by that friend, who did, however, help substantially afterwards.

On Whitmonday, 1930, about a thousand people from all parts of Wales gathered to commemorate the sixth anniversary of the College and the dedication of Derwen Fawr. On the grounds in front of the house is a large stone pedestal about four feet in height upon which a statue had been mounted. The statue was removed and on either side of the pedestal are those two scriptural statements as a permanent witness to God's faithfulness—''Jehovah-Jireh'' and ''Faith is Substance.''

28

Third Estate and Children's Home

While Mr. Howells was still paying for the Derwen Fawr estate and constantly looking to the Lord for the daily needs of the College, God's word came to go forward and erect new buildings. The first two to be built were a College Chapel to seat 200, and a Conference Hall to hold 400. Then came two men's dormitories and a women's dormitory to house a hundred students, all at a cost of about £6,000.

At the time the workmen were engaged, again there was not a penny in hand; but although they were regularly employed for over eighteen months, entailing a weekly wage of between £20 and £30, not once did they go away without receiving full pay. Even so, on Friday it was a rare thing to have money in hand for Saturday's wages. Sometimes the deliverance would not come by the first post on Saturday, calling for prevailing prayer before the second. "The Lord kept me daily and hourly abiding," said Mr. Howells, "to fulfill the condition for claiming an answer to my prayers."

During those months he was led for the first time to pray for a gift of £1,000. On a Tuesday morning, the Lord told him to stop all the workmen, put the lectures off, and devote every hour to waiting upon God. The work was not to restart until the £1,000 was sent, and during those days "there was not the sound of a hammer." Day by day they "prayed up and up, touching the Throne with every prayer," until on Friday morning the £1,000 came. "What a shout of victory there was in the camp!"

Each morning, when the milkman made his early call at the College, Mr. Howells was up to greet him. He used to say that, like himself, Mr. Howells had discovered the secret that "you have to be an early bird if you want to get on in the world!" When he arrived on the morning after the big lift, he put his cans down in deliberate fashion and, hands on hips, asked Mr. Howells, "Is it true what I've heard?" "What have you heard?" "That you've had a thousand pounds!" "Yes, it's quite true." "Well! well!! It seems that you and Amy Johnson [the aviator] are the only two that can get money these days!"

The building program was nearing an end when the next call came, in 1932. Mr. Howells was reading the life of Dr. Whitfield Guinness of the China Inland Mission, and how no one had offered a home to his children in Great Britain during their school holidays, although his parents had opened their home to so many people. He said that that cost him more heart agony than any persecutions endured in China.

The Lord used this to bring before Mr. Howells the need of many missionaries who have to leave their children in the homeland. It was one of the deep and agonizing experiences of his life. The pangs of the mothers who left their children in this country, with no home and no parents near, actually came on him; the Holy Spirit put them on him. He was in his room without food or sleep and his groans were heard, till he cried to the Lord, "What do You want *me* to do?" (He used to say there was a law—when you can carry a burden no longer, the Holy Spirit must take it.) He only came free when the Lord said to him, "I want you to make a home for every child of a missionary who cannot take his children back to the field," and he consented.

A deep experience, yes, and a great outcome. Out of the travail came the vision of the Home and School for missionaries' children, the fruit of that intercession gained years before, when God told him He had made him "a father to the orphans." From that day there was continued prayer in the

College, pleading the cause of mothers and fathers who have proved by their obedience that they love the Lord more than their own children.

To establish the Home, Rees Howells negotiated for several months with the Swansea Corporation about buying Sketty Park, the mansion of Sir Byng Morris, with seventeen acres of land, not far from the College. But in the end, the Corporation decided not to sell.

The next day, Sketty Isaf came on the market. This also was an estate of seventeen acres, just on the opposite side of the road to Derwen Fawr. The owners were willing to sell the house with five acres only, giving the option of purchase on the other twelve. The tenant was Major Pratt, who, when he heard that Mr. Howells had begun praying about it, said jokingly in his club, "If Rees Howells has begun looking over my wall and praying, I had better get out before something happens to me!"—and he did!

The Lord told Rees to buy it. The contract was drawn up by the agent and given him to sign, but he didn't have the deposit, so for three weeks he carried the document about in his pocket. The agent wanted it back, but Mr. Howells kept out of his way! In three weeks, however, the Lord delivered him, and Sketty Isaf was bought for £3,000. Only in a falling market, in days of depression, could such a house and grounds have been bought at so low a price, just as Derwen Fawr came into his hands at far below its value in a normal market. Later he bought the other twelve acres, and a further seven of adjoining freehold land.

The failure to buy Sketty Park, and then the Lord's guidance to the much more convenient estate of Sketty Isaf, illustrates an important lesson of faith, which Mr. Howells explained like this: "You are always getting a death on a point that is not really essential, and then receiving a better thing for it. Thus, before I bought Derwen Fawr, I was trying for months to buy another large place some miles away. We climbed up to the position of faith from which we could buy it, then my offer was refused—and I knew God was behind it. That very week

Derwen Fawr came onto the market, and I wouldn't change Derwen Fawr for two like that other estate.

"Then I came up to the position to buy Sketty Park. The moment the Corporation turned down my offer, what joy I had, because I recognized that God was in it; and the next day, Sketty Isaf came on the market!" Then he went on to mention how he tried to buy Sketty Hall, the home of Lord Swansea, but was turned down after climbing up in faith. (This incident is recorded in chapter 33.) In place of that property, the Lord told him to buy Penllergaer, and probably that great estate is worth several times as much as Sketty Hall.

This same principle of faith was to be seen in operation on many other occasions in his life. In pursuit of some great aim which the Lord had given him he would, en route, seek and ask and believe for some particular deliverance or provision which he would obtain, but not in the exact form in which he asked for it. To those who were watching from outside, this would often appear a failure or mistake, provoking much criticism. But the effect on him—and those on the inside with him in the battle of faith—was just the opposite: it only strengthened him in the pursuit of the main objective of faith until he had obtained it. He would regard a temporary disappointment en route not as a failure but as a stepping stone—rather like a climber who scales a peak mistakenly thinking it is the summit, only to find higher ones beyond and to find his determination increased to reach it. The same principle will be seen at work later in the great war-time battles of faith.

The Bible College at this time had about fifty students. Some of the earlier ones had by now been called to the staff: Tommy Howells, Mr. Howells' friend from Brynamman, Miss Margaret Williams and others taking various posts of responsibility. Among the tutors was the Rev. A. E. Glover, M.A., the author of *A Thousand Miles of Miracle*. Still other students were going to the mission fields with different societies: a couple with the China Inland Mission, a number with the Worldwide Evangelization Crusade, one student back to Mr. Howells' old station of Rusitu with the South Africa

General Mission, and a number of students into the home ministry.

The School for missionaries' children opened in 1933 with eleven boys and girls, including some day pupils from the surrounding district who were also accepted. With its development, care was taken to preserve the Home as a real home for the children without the intrusion of the school atmosphere. Numbers soon increased of both day scholars and missionaries' children, and God began to send the staff: Kenneth McDouall, M.A., as headmaster and Miss Doris Ruscoe, B.A., as headmistress, Miss G. Roderick as matron and mother to the children, Miss Elaine Bodley, headmistress of the Preparatory School, and other teachers and assistants, all giving their services freely to the Lord.

In 1935 the School moved down to Glynderwen, and with its rapid development, further extensions became necessary. A dormitory block, three blocks of classrooms, and a gymnasium were added. As usual, there was not a penny in hand when the builders arrived, the Lord not delivering for the first week's wages until the second post on Saturday, when a check of £20 came. The following Saturday the Lord moved a lady to leave the preparation of her dinner and come down to the College with £25! In ways like these, week by week, all the new buildings of the College and School, worth about £30,000, were erected on the three estates.

While they were putting up these extra buildings, Mr. Howells received nine separate gifts of £1,000. At one time the Lord told him that out of all gifts of £100 and over, he was to give away 25 per cent. One year he gave £1,000 to God's work elsewhere, although actually in need of it himself for this advance work. Rees always believed the law of the hundredfold, and acted on it. He began the College with 2s., and in fourteen years the Lord sent him £125,000.

During these years, besides the blessing that came to many visitors who already knew the Lord, there was a continual succession of people being led to the Savior, either through the College meetings or by coming under the the influence of the

Spirit through the very atmosphere of the place. Indeed, it would take a volume to tell the many stories of how "this and that man was born there" (Ps. 87:5).

29

The Book of Common Prayer and King Edward VIII

During the earlier years of the College there were some outstanding examples of answers to prayer on a national scale. They were the precursors of the strategic praying on a worldwide scale to which the College was to be called in later years. Two of them are worth recording.

The controversy which raged over the proposed introduction of the new Book of Common Prayer in the Church of England in 1928 will well be remembered. Practically all the bishops were in favor of it, despite its Romeward tendencies; and according to the newspapers, it was a foregone conclusion that Parliament would accept it. There must have been very few in the country who could have believed that the House of Commons would reject it.

Suddenly, two days before the debate in the House, the Holy Spirit asked Mr. Howells if he believed the Lord could stop it going through. If he did, he was to call a meeting that afternoon for the one definite purpose of "turning down the new Book of Common Prayer." He fought it out alone with God from 10 a.m. to 1 p.m. and then called the meeting. Lectures for the afternoon were canceled. The Spirit came down with great power, and the meeting continued until the Lord gave full assurance of victory.

The next morning the newspapers told how the House of Lords had voted and accepted it; but the veto was with the House of Commons, who were to vote that day. The Holy Spirit said to Mr. Howells, "Go on, nothing doubting." The dramatic scenes in the House of Commons will be remembered when, before a crowded audience, one or two members spoke as they had never spoken before on the dangers of allowing any further Romeward tendencies to creep into the national Church. It was reported that the atmosphere of the House was like a religious meeting, and to the amazement of everybody, they voted the new Book of Common Prayer out. But, as Mr. Howells explained, "The Lord had given us the victory the previous afternoon."

Some years later, in 1936, there came the serious national crisis over King Edward VIII and his proposed marriage to Mrs. Wallis Simpson, an American divorcee. In this again the Lord led the College to take a stand in prayer. The diaries of the daily meetings give the following account:

December 4. "The news about the king has come to light in the morning papers, and the Director tells us how serious conditions are. We came back in the evening and pleaded with the Lord to guide the king, and give wisdom and discernment to all those concerned in this crisis."

December 5. "Day of prayer in College. Situation in England very grave, because it concerns not only our land but the British Empire."

December 6. "Day of prayer and fasting in the College. We pray for the Empire in its present crisis. The Lord reveals that it is His will for Edward to abdicate. Mr. Howells was as strong as a lion in the fight and declared, 'Edward is *not* to reign, or the Lord has not spoken by me.' There is a wonderful victory as we believe in the evening."

December 7. "There is thanksgiving over the victory of yesterday. The papers reveal that while at the end of last week the king was challenging the position, now he is anxious to do only what will be best for the Empire."

December 9. "Believing for the Lord to help King Edward to make decision according to God's will, and that his soul may be blessed."

December 10. "Came back at 2:30 p.m. to ask the Lord to control the country, now that the news of the abdication of King Edward VIII is known."

December 11. "We are thankful for this believing of the Holy Spirit. The Lord has saved the Empire and raised the standard of life in our beloved land."

The College had a growing company of friends in South Wales getting great spiritual refreshment from the meetings and fellowship. Many were frequent visitors and faithful supporters of the work. To some, also, Mr. Howells was able to minister in things practical as well as spiritual.

One man, who had been a friend of the College since its foundation, went through very hard trials in his business. His creditors were pressing him, and one day, in desperation, he asked Mr. Howells to pray that the Lord would take the wheels off their chariots (Ex. 14:25)! This friend was to the point of locking the door and giving up everything. "You will do nothing of the sort," Rees instructed. "What about your sons?" Mr. Howells then took him to the bank and arranged to clear all he needed. From that day he began to prosper, and was the means of much blessing to the College for many years.

There was another friend of the College, a deacon in Rees Howells' church, who used to come to the meetings. After his business went down he came with a very heavy heart to talk things over with Mr. Howells and ask for prayer. One day Mr. Howells went to his home and found that everything was being sold! The mother and daughter were crying. But the Lord told His servant to tell them *he* was going to meet the demands on them. Immediately the tears became tears of joy!

Another time Mr. Howells was needing money for the property taxes. He also knew of a man who was in the same position, and the last day had come for them both. Mr. Howells had not nearly enough for his own need, which was £40, but he did have the £8 needed by his friend. So he went to give it to him.

When he arrived, he found the man and his wife on their

knees praying for the money. "You can get up from your knees," he said. "The Lord has told me to deliver you." He said nothing about his own need, but on his return to the College he found a gift waiting for him—of £40!

On another occasion Mr. Howells was praying for a certain sum of money which he needed that very day. There was a woman who always gave him that amount at this particular season, in the middle of the term. This time, however, she arrived on that very day and brought the deliverance. But Mr. Howells could see she was cast down. She told him that her son-in-law was in great trouble, and that there was a case in the courts over it. If he had committed the crime and was found guilty, he would be imprisoned. The case was coming up in a week, and she couldn't sleep. She wanted Mr. Howells to go to the Lord about it and then tell her whether he would be put in prison or not.

"I had prayed for that money and she had brought it," he said, "and that might sway my judgment. Could the Lord tell me whether he was guilty or not? I wondered. If he was guilty, the Lord couldn't make him free. On the other hand, if he was not guilty and was in danger of being committed, could the Lord deliver him?

"I went upstairs and was there a long time. After much prayer, the Lord told me, 'He is not guilty and he will be freed.' So I asked her, 'Did *the Lord* send you today? Did *He* tell you I would give you the result?' 'Yes,' she said. So I said to her, 'If you want to cry, cry all you want to now before I tell you; but you are not to shed one tear after. He is not guilty, and he will be freed!' "

To their surprise, the jury could not agree and they had to postpone the case for two days. Then, when the case was resumed, the judge found one of the witnesses telling a somewhat different story from before. The prosecution broke down and the judge at once stopped the case. The man was acquitted, and the news went all through the town.

30

The Every Creature Commission

The autumn of 1934 was a wonderful time in the College. In the early morning Mr. Howells was spending many hours alone with God, going through the four Gospels, and getting great light from the Holy Spirit on the Life and Person of the Savior. He seemed to be coming to the morning meetings straight from God's presence, and Mrs. Howells, who knew the Spirit's ways with him, was conscious that the Lord was preparing him for something.

On Boxing Day morning (December 26), the Spirit began speaking to him even earlier than usual, before he had arisen. Mrs. Howells, who was also awake, heard him repeating, "every creature, every creature." At 3 a.m. he was so conscious that God wanted to say something definite to him that he dressed and went to his room downstairs. There the Lord asked him if he believed the Savior meant His last command to be obeyed.

"I do," he replied. "Then do you believe that I can give the gospel to every creature?" "Without stretching a point," he answered, "I believe You can. You are God." "I am dwelling in you," the Lord then said. "Can I be responsible for this through you?"

For years Mr. Howells had been praying for the gospel to go to the world. Before he went to Africa, the Spirit brought before him God's promise to His Son in Psalm 2:8. He had not let a day pass without praying that the Savior should have "the heathen for His inheritance and the uttermost parts of the earth for His possession," and it was in willingness to be, in some measure, the answer to his own prayers that he had accepted the call to Africa.

Then, while in Africa, he had been struck by Andrew Murray's comment on the Savior's word in Matthew 9:38, "Pray ye therefore the Lord of the harvest that He will send forth laborers into His harvest." Andrew Murray had pointed out, on the strength of this verse, that the number of missionaries on the field depends entirely on the extent to which someone obeys that command and prays out the laborers; and the Lord had called Mr. Howells to do this. That, in turn, had been one of God's ways of preparing him for the further commission to start a Bible College. Thus, for years he had been a man with a world vision.

But this new word from God was to lay direct responsibility on *him*. It was no mere assent to the general command to preach the gospel to every creature. It meant, if accepted, that he and all who took it with him would be bond-servants for the rest of their days to this one task—to intercede, to go, to serve others who go—to be responsible for seeing that every creature hears the gospel.

The way this commission was interpreted to Mr. Howells in concrete terms was that in the next thirty years the Holy Ghost would find 10,000 channels from all over the world—men and women whom He would enter and who would allow Him to take complete possession of them for this task, even as years before He had taken possession of His servant.

Finance would be needed in abundance, but the One who gave millions to David for the temple could give the same to those who were building a far more precious temple, a building not made with hands, eternal in the heavens. He gave His servant that word in Deuteronomy 28:12 (RV, margin): "The Lord shall open unto thee His good treasury . . . and thou shalt lend unto many nations"; and with the word was the promise of a first gift from "the Treasury" of £10,000, which was to be a confirmation.

Rees Howells came out from his room a man with a vision and a burden which never left him—the "Every Creature Vision." He brought it before the staff and students, and New Year's Day 1935 was given to prayer and fasting. The presence of God was felt in a very real way and, while they did not minimize the enormity of the task, a deep and growing conviction took possession of many that God was going to do a new thing. It was a conviction that as really as the Savior came down to the world to make an atonement for every creature, so the Holy Ghost had come down to make that atonement known to every creature, and that He would complete it in their generation.

In a new sense the world began to be their parish. They began to be open for God to lay any prayer on them which would further the reaching of every creature with the gospel. They became responsible to intercede for countries and nations, as well as for individual missionaries and societies. The College truly became "a house of prayer for all nations."

One form that this prayer warfare took was intercession on a national and international level concerning anything that affected world evangelization. Every creature must hear, therefore the doors must be kept open.

Their prayers became strategic. They must face and fight the enemy wherever he was opposing freedom to evangelize. God was preparing an instrument—a company to fight world battles on their knees.

The first battle of prayer on this international scale was in 1936 when Germany sent her soldiers into the Rhineland and broke the Locarno Treaty. "We knew that France would be on fire in a day," said Mr. Howells, "and it meant nothing less than a European war, and the consequent hindrance to the spread of the gospel. Only those who were in the College can realize the burden the Holy Spirit put on us. 'Prevail against Hitler,' He said to me, and it meant three weeks of prayer and fasting."

The daily diary of the College meetings at that time records:

March 21. "Things are very black on the Continent. We pray on until 11 a.m., and come back at 2:30, 6 and 9 p.m. We ask the Lord to deal with Germany."

March 23. "Very grave on Continent and in London. Meetings at 9 and 11 a.m., and 6 and 9 p.m. We plead with God to deal with Hitler and the German nation, and to bring them to account."

March 24. "Situation regarding European crisis very black, all the countries are disagreeing with each other. Burden is coming on very heavy, but the Lord is allowing us to plead the Every Creature Vision in His presence. The Lord turns our eyes off the countries to Himself. Meetings at 9 a.m., 6 and 9 p.m."

It continued like that for another five days. Then on March 29 Mr. Howells came into the meeting and said, "Prayer has failed. We are on slippery ground. Only intercession will avail. God is calling for intercessors—men and women who will lay their lives on the altar to fight the devil, as really as they would have to fight the enemy on the western front." It was made clear that a soldier at the front has no say in where he goes and what he does; he cannot take holidays or attend to the claims of home and loved ones, as other people can; and the Lord was telling them that if, as really as that, some would become bond-slaves to the Holy Spirit for every creature, and would throw their lives into the gap (Ezek. 22:30), He would give the victory and avert war. A large number of the staff and students made the surrender. "We came right through," said Mr. Howells, "and I knew from that time on Hitler was no more than a rod in the hands of the Holy Spirit." The diary recorded:

March 29. "The most wonderful day in the College so far. Big day of surrenders, and many take up the challenge of martyrdom."

March 30. "Fire fell on sacrifice. Holy Ghost descended on evening meeting. Went on knees and someone started the chorus, 'Welcome, welcome, welcome! Holy Ghost, we welcome Thee.' Liberty and power so great we continued singing this one chorus for a full hour."

April 1. "Another day of worshiping and praising the Lord. He has come down on the College, and it is a new place; there is singing from Derwen Fawr to Glynderwen."

From that Sunday onwards, the crisis of war in Europe changed into a search for peace. When the proposal was made for a twenty-five year Peace Pact, the College also had the assurance that they could prevail on God to keep his hand on Hitler and the Nazi menace. Every time he made a new swoop, such as on Austria, days were set aside for prayer. The greatest test came in the summer of 1938 when the dispute arose with Hitler over Czechoslovakia, resulting in what became known as the Munich Crisis.

We now know that the voice Hitler followed, which coincided with the advice of some of his trusted advisors, was urging him to attack while Britain was still totally unprepared. War seemed inescapable, and the leaders of the nation called for a day of prayer. God made the challenge very real to the College and for days the conflict was bitter. It was essentially a clash of spiritual forces—a test of strength between the devil in Hitler and the Holy Ghost in His army of intercessors.

At the height of the battle the one prayer that the Holy Ghost gave to the College through His servant was, "Lord, bend Hitler." A point came when that cry of travail changed into a shout of victory. The devil had to give way.

It was just before the commencement of the new session in the College, and the victory was so certain that Mr. Howells turned the opening day into a day of praise. An announcement appeared in the *South Wales Evening Post* on Saturday, September 17, stating that "The meetings [of the following Thursday] will take the form of Praise and Thanksgiving because God has again averted a European War."

Hundreds gathered in the Conference Hall in that dark hour to join in praising God. In the days that followed, the test ran higher and higher, but faith was steadfast and on Thursday, September 29, the College and School were given a general holiday, to celebrate the coming victory. The next day, September 30, the Munich Pact was signed. War had been averted!

But what *did* happen to Hitler? The one person who was in a position to know was Sir Neville Henderson, the British Ambassador to Germany at that fateful time. In his book *Failure of a Mission* he makes the following significant statements in describing the remarkable reaction in Hitler after signing the Munich Pact:

> Hitler felt irritated with himself. A section of his followers were always egging him on to fight England while [England] was militarily unprepared. They reproached him for having accepted the Munich settlement and thus having missed the most favorable opportunity. An uneasy feeling lest they might have been right contributed to Hitler's ill-humor. . . . His Voice told him that . . . there could be no more propitious moment for a [war] than that October; and for once he had been obliged to disregard that Voice and to listen to counsels of prudence. . . . For the first time he had failed to obey his Voice. . . . He had acted on several occasions in direct defiance of the advice of his stoutest followers and of his army, yet the event had always proved him to be right. Until Munich. There, for the first time, he had been compelled to listen to contrary opinion, and his own faith in his Voice and his people's confidence in his judgement were for the first time shaken. . . . "You are the only man," he said somewhat bitterly to Mr. Chamberlain, "to whom I have ever made a concession."[1]

The Lord had "bent" Hitler.

It was certainty of this victory, and the knowledge that the Holy Ghost was stronger than the devil in Hitler, that enabled the College to take the assurance a year later, when war did come, that that was not the triumph of Satan but it was "God's war on the Beast."

One thing that also strengthened Mr. Howells and his followers very much in their challenge of faith at that time was the fact that in July 1938, shortly before this crisis, God had given His promised seal on the Every Creature Vision—the gift of £10,000!

[1]Neville Henderson, *Failure of a Mission*, pp. 175-6, 179, 157: Hodder and Stoughton, Ltd. Quoted by permission of the author's executors.

31

Ethiopia

Soon after the crisis of March 1936 came the fight for Ethiopia. It was hard and long, and seemed to end in dismal failure. As soon as it was apparent that Mussolini intended to invade the country, Mr. Howells and the College saw what lay behind it.

Ethiopia, through the influence of the Emperor, was opening in a new way to evangelical missions and there was a prospect of widespread evangelization in many areas. Mr. Howells realized that once again it was a campaign against the enemy in the Church of Rome, for if Italy captured the country it would be the end of the Protestant witness there.

The battle of intercession lasted for three weeks. "It was as if we were fighting in the country itself," said Mr. Howells. "We believed that God would not give Ethiopia to the Fascist dictator." The fight became fiercest when the Italian army began to get near the capital, Addis Ababa. The College journal for those days in 1936 reported:

April 24. "Day of prayer and fasting (except for breakfast). Great burden as we pray for the Ethiopians. It gets really hard towards the evening and news in the paper is very serious. We are believing the Italians will not enter Addis Ababa."

April 25. "Four meetings of prayer. There is a big burden to be carried. We are believing that the Lord will intervene and give the Italians a setback."

April 28. "The burden is great. Many feel assured that the Italians will not enter Addis Ababa and the whole College is coming up to believe this big thing."

April 29. "We are coming up in solid faith to take hold of the Lord to stop the Italians."

May 1. "The fight still very fierce. We had three wonderful hours with the Lord pleading for the hundred missionaries in the capital. *The Lord tells the Director that he is to go back from public life for the next ten years and intercede for the nations.* Oh, the joy of being in this life and taking part in the battle of intercession!"

May 4. "Day of prayer and fasting; there is a big burden for Addis Ababa, as we read of the rioting which started when the Emperor left the palace. Hard day, but we are believing the Lord is going to intervene, although He is allowing the test to run very high."

May 5. "Still big burden for Addis Ababa. Italians march in at 4 p.m. this afternoon."

It was the first lesson for many in the College of what we have seen a number of times in Mr. Howells's life, namely, the death in an intercession which has to precede the resurrection, and the test on the intercessors as to whether they can walk through their valley of humiliation, of apparent failure, with an unmoved faith. The very thing they believed for did not come to pass. The Italians were not to occupy the capital, but they did so, and the Emperor was a fugitive. Rome had triumphed. It seemed the end of gospel work in the country. But Mr. Howells explained to the College the principle that has already been referred to (p. 197): that apparent failure may only be a steppingstone to greater victory. The College record continues:

May 6. "The Director has more light on intercession to show us—that unless we had interceded for those men in Ethiopia, we would never have suffered with them; and if our prayers were of faith, we have only had a setback and not a failure as the result of unbelief. Great public meeting at 7:30 p.m., when the Holy Ghost revealed to us Joseph 'the dreamer' who stood to what God had shown him and went through tremendous testings, but finally saw what he believed come to pass.''

In order to keep the story of God's dealings with the College concerning Ethiopia as one whole, we will rapidly review the happenings of the next few years, although it takes us well beyond the date we have at present reached.

Although the day had come when Mussolini had captured the country, the College never lost faith. The Emperor came to England, and then, of all the unlikely things, came to the College. Who but God could have directed his steps to the company of people who had probably prayed in more concentrated fashion than any others for him and his people?

It happened that Alfred Buxton, C.T. Studd's son-in-law, who was leader of the Bible Churchmen's Missionary Society in Ethiopia, knew that the College had a home and school for missionaries' children. He wrote to Mr. Howells to ask if he would take into the school Lidj Asrate Kassa, the son of Ras Kassa and a relative of the Emperor. (He later became known as Dejazmach Asrate Kassa, and became Governor-General of one of the large provinces of Ethiopia.)

A year later the Emperor himself asked if he could come and visit the College and see Asrate. He was given a civic welcome in Swansea by the Mayor and Mayoress, Councilor David Richards and his daughter, and taken to the Guildhall, where he signed the Visitors' Book. The Mayor, in addressing him, said that he was still "Your Majesty" to him, and he believed to the people of Swansea, and they hoped that some day he would be restored to his country. Only God could do that, he added. The Emperor then visited the College and School, where he had tea.

Mr. Howells had just bought the mansion in Penllergaer, and he offered it to the Emperor for his residence in England, until their prayer was answered and he was back on his throne. As they drove up the avenue of over a mile, ablaze with rhododendrons and azaleas, tears were in the Emperor's eyes, and he remarked to Mrs. Howells, "If heaven is a more beautiful place than this, it must be very wonderful. What your husband has done reminds me of an Ethiopian proverb: 'The man who has only God to look to can do all things and never fail.'" The Emperor was also much moved to hear how Mr. Howells had been called to help the Jewish refugees because, as he said, "I am a refugee myself."

A few days later he wrote:

Haile Selassie I
Elect of God, Emperor of Ethiopia

To Rev. and Mrs. Rees Howells,

It is with profound gratitude that I want to write to you to-day to thank you most heartily for all the kindness you have shown me during my visit to your Bible College last week. It is an inspiration to me to have seen all the wonderful things that the Lord has been leading you to do among those of your own people and those who have found a refuge in your country. I do pray that God in His grace will continue to bless this great work of His very richly.

Sincerely yours,

(Signed personally by the Emperor).

The Emperor's private chaplain, and his son-in-law, Abye Abebe, now Brigadier-General and Minister of War, came to the College for a period as students. In the summer of 1939 the Emperor himself spent a fortnight in camp in the Penllergaer grounds, and came down each night to the meeting in the College. By the end of his stay, the outbreak of war was imminent and he went straight back from the camp to London, and later from London to his own country. In June 1941, when the Emperor re-entered his capital, he sent Mr. Howells this cable:

You will, I know, share in my joy at entering my capital. I send you this telegram in remembrance of past sympathy and help.

Emperor Haile Selassie.

To which Mr. Howells replied:

Thank you for telegram. Praising God daily for restoring Ethiopia and giving back your throne. The Lord bless and keep you and give you peace.

Rees Howells, Bible College, Swansea.

God's answer was perfect. The expansion of missionary work in the country since the expulsion of the Italians has been by far the greatest in its history. Just as it was to be later in the World War, so now, the answer to the intercession could not have been complete until the aggressor had been so dealt with that he could not rise up and menace the country again; and when the missionaries returned, it was reported in the Walamo district that they could not account for the revival which had been actually going on during the Italian occupation, when some 500 converts had increased to 20,000!

32

Visitation of the Spirit

From the time of special dedication on March 29, 1936, when so many of the College (both staff and students) laid their lives on the altar as intercessors, the Spirit was at work in the College. The climax and consummation came in the New Year of 1937. It was the "Pentecost" of the College, from which they emerged, not a loosely-linked company of consecrated individuals, but a body in the full sense of the term—a living, integrated organism, infused with one life and one purpose. Dr. Kingsley C. Priddy, M.B., B.S., D.T.M.&H., a member of the staff and later headmaster of the school, gives the following account of those days:

"In the Christmas vacation of 1936 much time was given to prayer. As we approached the new year of 1937 there was an increasing consciousness of God's presence. The first outward sign that He was working in a new way was when one of the staff broke down in prayer, confessing her sense of need and crying to the Holy Spirit to meet her. Then we heard how the Holy Ghost had so manifested Himself in the glory of His Divine Person to some of the girl students that they wept before Him for hours—broken at the corruption of their own hearts revealed in the light of His holiness.

"An awesome sense of God's nearness began to steal over the whole College. There was a solemn expectancy. We were reminded of the 120 in the Upper Room before the day of

Pentecost. Like them, we only wanted to spend our time 'in prayer and supplication'—conscious that God's hand was upon us—conscious that He was about to do something. God was there; yet we felt we were still waiting for Him to come. And in the days that followed, *He came.*

"He did not come like a rushing mighty wind. But gradually the person of the Holy Ghost filled all our thoughts, His presence filled all the place, and His light seemed to penetrate all the hidden recesses of our hearts. He was speaking through the Director in every meeting, but it was in the quiet of our own rooms that He revealed Himself to many of us.

"We felt the Holy Spirit had been a real Person to us before; as far as we knew we had received Him; and some of us had known much of His operations in and through our lives. But now the revelation of His Person was so tremendous that all our previous experiences seemed as nothing. There was no visible apparition, but He made Himself so real to our spiritual eyes that it was a 'face to face' experience. And when we saw Him we knew we had never really seen Him before. We said like Job, 'I have heard of Thee by the hearing of the ear: but now mine eye seeth Thee'; and like him, we cried, 'Wherefore I abhor myself and repent in dust and ashes.'

"In the light of His purity, it was not so much *sin* we saw as *self*. We saw pride and self-motives underlying everything we had ever done. Lust and self-pity were discovered in places where we had never suspected them. And we had to confess we knew nothing of the Holy Ghost as an indwelling Person. That our bodies were meant to be the temples of the Holy Ghost we knew, but when He pressed the question, 'Who is living in *your* body?' we could not say that *He* was. We would have done so once, but now we had *seen* Him.

"In His nature He was just like Jesus—He would never live for self, but always for others. We were people who had left all to follow the Savior, and had forsaken all we had of this world's goods to enter a life of faith, and as far as we knew we had surrendered our lives entirely to the One who died for us. But He showed us, 'There is all the difference in the world between *your* surrendered life in My hands, and Me living *My* life in your body.'

"We read the Acts afresh and found we were reading, not the acts of the apostles, but the acts of the Holy Ghost. The bodies of Peter and the others had become His temples. The Holy Ghost as a divine Person lived in the bodies of the apostles, even as the Savior had lived His earthly life in the body that was born in Bethlehem. And all that the Holy Spirit asked of us was our wills and our bodies.

" 'I beseech you therefore, brethren, by the mercies of God, that ye present your bodies a living sacrifice . . .' (Rom. 12:1). It seemed as though we had never seen that Scripture before. He made it clear that He was not asking for service, but for a sacrifice. 'Our God is a consuming fire'; and if God the Holy Ghost took possession of these bodies, then *His* life was going to consume all that there was of *ours*.

"We had often sung 'I want to be like Jesus,' but when we had the offer from a Person who is just like the Savior to come and live that life daily and hourly in us, we found how unreal we had been. How much there was in us that still wanted to live our own lives—that shrank from this 'sentence of death'! We now began to see the meaning of the Savior's words in Luke 9:24, 'For whosoever will save his life shall lose it: but whosoever will lose his life for My sake, the same shall save it.'

"Why had He manifested Himself to us in this way? He made that quite clear. It was because there was a work to be done in the world today that only He could do (John 16:8). No wonder the Master told His disciples not to move from Jerusalem until they had received 'the promise of the Father.' But when He had come, they would be His witnesses 'in Jerusalem, and in all Judaea, and in Samaria, and unto the uttermost part of the earth.'

"Many of us on the previous March 29 had put our all on the altar for the sake of giving the gospel to every creature. We had become willing to be any cog in the machinery that God needed to put that through in our generation. But now the Holy Ghost said, as Jehovah had said to Moses, 'I am come down to do it.' And we knew that He was as almighty as He was holy.

"As those days of visitation went on, we were just prostrate at His feet. We had thought that there was some virtue in our surrender: that we, with thousands of others, would be the people to evangelize the world in this generation. But now *He* had come, and we were out of it—except in so far as our bodies would become the temples in which He would dwell and through which He would work. He said, 'I have not come to give you joy, or peace, or victory. I have not come to give you any blessing at all. You will find all that you need in Jesus. But I have come to put *you* to the cross, so that I may live in your body for the sake of a lost world' (Col. 3:3; 2 Cor. 4:10; Gal. 2:20).

"He warned us that the trials before this task was through would be so great, and the attacks of Satan so fierce, that 'flesh and blood' would never be able to hold out. He showed us that on the eve of the crucifixion, when the real clash came with the powers of darkness, it was only the Savior who stood. We saw every one of the disciples fail in that hour—in spite of all their surrenders, their vows and their devotion to the Master. And looking into the future years—the darkness of the last days of this age, the final contest between heaven and hell for the kingdoms of this world—we could see only One Person who was 'sufficient for these things,' and He was the glorious Third Person of the Godhead in those whom He was able to indwell.

"One by one He met us; one by one we broke in tears and contrition before Him. From one after another rose the cry, as it did from Isaiah when he too 'saw the Lord': 'Woe is *me* for *I* am undone . . . unclean.' One by one our wills were broken; we yielded on *His own* unconditional terms. To one by one there came the glorious realization: *He had entered*, and the wonder of our privilege just overwhelmed us.

"The personal experience was great. We were new people. His Word became new. So often we had had to water down the Word to the level of our experience. But now the Person in us would insist on bringing our experience up to the level of His Word. We understood that crucifixion was a slow death, and that He would have much to deal with in us before He would really be free to do His work through us. But one thing we knew—He had come and He could never fail.

"But far greater than anything His visitation could mean to us personally was what it was going to mean to the world. We saw Him as the One to whom 'the nations are as a drop of a bucket, and are counted as the small dust of the balance.' On our faces before Him we could only say, from awed hearts, 'Holy Ghost, You have come to shake the world.'

"There was no excitement or enthusiasm of the flesh in those days. When His power had come upon us after March 29 we had been carried away and were singing and shouting our praises. But in these days we were so awed by the holy majesty of His Person that we hardly dared raise our voices in the meetings.

"Even the grounds outside seemed filled with His presence. Walking around together we would suddenly be conscious that we were speaking in whispers. The late hours came, but no one thought of bed—for God was there. It seemed to be a foretaste of the Holy City: 'There shall be no night there.' 2 and 3 a.m. often seemed just like midday as we communed together, prayed with some who were 'coming through,' or waited before God in the quietness of our hearts.

"His visitation lasted for some three weeks in this *special* sense although, praise God, He came to 'abide,' and has continued with us ever since. But no one has a monopoly of the Holy Ghost. He is God, and whatever our experience of Him, He is far greater than all we can know of Him. Whatever we know of His gifts, His manifestations and His anointings, He is greater than all those. In whatever way He has manifested Himself to us, we also recognize His mighty working in and through others. Increasingly we look to the Holy Ghost Himself, poured out on all flesh as Joel prophesied, as the only One by whom the Vision He has shown us can be fulfilled, through His prepared channels, in all parts of the world."

Through this falling of the fire upon the sacrifice the Spirit had sealed to Himself a company of intercessors for every creature. Tutors and school teachers, doctors and nurses, domestic and office workers, gardeners and mechanics: their duties were varied but their commission one. Many of the students themselves remained on as part of this praying and working company. There are times in God's dealings with His servants when He sets apart for Himself not just individuals but companies—baptized, as it were, by one Spirit into one body for one God-appointed purpose — and this was now one of them.

33

Fourth Estate and the Jews

The next burden which came on Mr. Howells was for the Jews. As we follow him and the College through their months and years of intercession for Israel, it is remarkable now to see the fulfillment of the first stage of their prayer in the actual return of the Jews and the establishment of the State of Israel. How little there seemed any outward sign that this would come to pass when the burden first came on God's servant! It reminds us that no great event in history, even though prophesied beforehand in the Scriptures, comes to pass unless God finds His human channels of faith and obedience. Prophecies must be believed into manifestation, as well as foretold.

The burden first came on Mr. Howells when he read of the proclamation by Italy, on September 3, 1938, that all Jews must clear out of Italy in six months. This, coupled with the anti-Semitism then so fierce in Germany, turned his thoughts towards the return of God's people to their own land. He said at the meetings:

September 3. "I have a great burden for these people, and I want God to lay their burden on me. The devil, through Hitler and Mussolini, is being used to send them back to their own land. It is the fulfillment of prophecy; it is another sign that this is the closing of the age. I am longing to help God's people to return to their land."

September 5. "In Isaiah's prophecies about the second

return of God's people, he says in chapters 11 and 12 that God will draw them from the four corners of the earth. That is just what is happening today. The Holy Spirit is longing to help them through someone. I want God to touch me deeper still with the feelings of what these people are suffering."

September 7. "Daniel was able to prevail with God in a wonderful way for the return of God's people, after he had seen that the seventy years of captivity were ended. We must have faith and believe God's covenant with Abraham that they are to dwell in the land, and not merely have sympathetic feelings for the Jews. God moved Cyrus—the one who had held them in captivity—to supply the money to take them back! He will do this again, if someone will believe Him. I firmly believe the times of the Gentiles are drawing to a close, and the Jews must be back in their own land when the Master returns."

September 11. "I think of the places of intercession gained for the tramps, in the village, as a Nazarite, for the widows of India, for a tubercular, for the missionaries' children. Now God is calling us to be responsible for the Jews."

He then began to describe how God had definitely told him to be responsible for a gift of £100,000 for the Jews, and to believe for it. Days were spent in believing prayer for this sum.

A few weeks later, however, news came of Hitler "throwing out" several thousand Jewish children on the Polish border, and the burden on Mr. Howells increased. "The moment I read this in the paper," he told the College, "a great anguish came over me. Nobody knows what this must mean to their parents. The Holy Ghost is just like a father, and if I were a father of children whose home had been destroyed, wouldn't I seek a shelter for them straight away? The Holy Ghost suffers like that for all those parents on the Continent. Unless He in you makes the suffering your own, you can't intercede for them. You will never touch the Throne unless you send up that real cry; words don't count at all."

As usual, when he had a burden like that, he felt sure that God would have him do something. As he asked what he could do, the answer came: "Make a home for them."

Rees Howells had already bought three estates by faith, but the Lord was now going to call him to a new and greater venture in finance. He tried to rent the home of Sir Percy Molyneux, a friend of his who had lately passed away. He calculated that he could house fifty children in it, but the owners were not willing to let him have it.

He then tried for a larger one, which would hold 250. Again he was turned down.

Then one night God whispered to him, "Penllergaer": the name of an estate he had heard of but never seen. He knew that it was one of the largest in the Swansea area, and that the owner was Sir Charles Llewelyn. On inquiry, he found that it consisted of 270 acres, and that the Roman Catholics had made a former offer of £14,000 for the mansion and two fields only; so he realized that it would cost him nothing less than £20,000.

The records of the meetings for the next week or two speak of constant prayer about it, until on November 26 he came right out with the statement: "I shall buy the new estate, probably next week, and I am willing to risk my all in order to help the Jews."

When Mr. Howells went to the agent he found that he had no time to lose, because some others were preparing to make an offer for it. He must make a decision in twenty-four hours. That day Rees Howells said at the meeting, "These others are forming a company to buy Penllergaer, and I must look to the Trinity to be my Company." And the day following: "Today I was told would be the last for buying Penllergaer, so I made an offer greater than that of the Syndicate. The agent told me it would be ours, and he is writing to the owner this evening."

The matter was settled. With some alterations that would be needed it was going to cost £20,000, and there was nothing in hand! This dwarfed the previous purchases of faith, but God had so led him on through the years that, where we might think the test would be tremendous (and it actually was), yet, as one of the students said, he bought

Penllergaer with less fuss than many a man makes in buying a suit of clothes! He was encouraged a few days later by a phone call from a very close friend of the College, who said that if Mr. Howells was staking his all on Penllergaer he would do the same, and that a freehold house given him by his father was to be sold for that purpose.

"Penllergaer was a marvelous estate, far exceeding any of the other three. There was a large mansion with many out-buildings, seven other dwelling houses, a home farm and market gardens where the late Sir John Llewelyn used to employ fifteen gardeners. The estate was famous for its collec-tion of trees and shrubs, and had been used by the Swansea University for student classes in Botany. The river and lake of eighteen acres were popular among fishermen for their trout. The beautiful drive up to the mansion, of a mile and a quarter in length, was through masses of rhododendrons and azaleas.

Here Mr. Howells had the vision of "the persecuted little ones" being driven up through these banks of rhododendrons ablaze with bloom and feeling they were more than halfway already to their home of destiny, the land of Palestine, which is yet to flow with milk and honey.

The papers referred to this "City of Refuge in Wales for Jewish Refugee Children," and the London papers gave it headlines also. Negotiations were opened with the Home Secretary for permission for several hundred Jewish children to be brought over. All this would mean much heavier financial liability and a guarantee of £50 would have to be paid down for each child.

God then called them to one more costly step—most costly of all. It concerned the £100,000 gift for which the College was praying. As Rees Howells said, "There is a golden rule in the life of faith, that the Christian can never prevail upon God to move others to give larger sums of money towards God's work than he himself has either given or proved that he is will-ing to give if it were in his power to do so."

On this basis God spoke to him for several days. There was then a great sensation in the College when, in a Sunday morning meeting, he told them what God was asking, and that he had made his decision. It was that they would sell all the three present estates, Glynderwen, Derwen Fawr and Sketty Isaf, which had been valued at close to £100,000, and give that as the first £100,000 for the Jews. The College and School would move to Penllergaer and occupy it together with the Jewish children.

Mrs. Howells had also been facing up to the sacrifice of all these estates with their hallowed associations, and the cost of having to build the work afresh in Penllergaer. It seemed unthinkable that God could really mean this, but when she heard her husband commit himself in public, she knew well that it was final.

Can we imagine her feelings as she left that meeting, her eyes blinded with tears? Alone with God she fought her battle. She missed the next meeting and also took no lunch, but by three o'clock God brought her right through as she saw Abraham walking up the mount with his son Isaac and offering him there as a whole burnt-offering to God. Without knowing how his wife had come through, Mr. Howells preached on that very passage of Scripture in the afternoon meeting. He asked her to close the meeting in prayer, and there were very few dry eyes in the congregation.

Negotiations then began for the sale of the estates. The army had already requisitioned some fields next to Derwen Fawr for training purposes and were making inquiries about the College properties. So Mr. Howells began to negotiate with the War Office about this sale. It was only after several months that the Western Command finally decided not to extend any further in this district, and the Lord did not test His servant more on that point.

At this same time there was a series of meetings in the College when the Lord spoke to many about laying their missionary calls on the altar and allowing the Holy Ghost, through them, to take the place of fathers and mothers to the Jewish refugee children. It was a real surrender on the part of many. And, although that ministry never materialized, it was God's strange way of wisdom, for it meant that this company of about 120 were set apart by the Holy Ghost during those unexpected war years for the life of intercession. Once again it was God using one apparent call to prepare His servants for another and higher. By this means He had His army of the Spirit, who were going to fight the war through on their knees to free the world again for every creature to hear the gospel.

While they were preparing to receive the children, war was declared with Germany and their plans had to be changed, although twelve Jewish children did arrive and became part of the College family. It was another testing time for Rees Howells. "When you try to do something for God, everything comes against you," he observed. "Could anything be more against me than this—that, after I bought Penllergaer for the children, the war came and I couldn't take them? But when God speaks to you, you can never doubt it. If what God has told you leads you into great trials, then you go back to God and turn the burden of it on Him.

"Nothing could have looked more like a mistake than this, for I had a great liability at that time, but I did not question it once. I knew it wasn't a mistake, although the devil told me it was. Although we could not get the children, yet we obeyed God in buying that property. He told us that we were to have thousands of pounds out of it to use for the Kingdom."

How wonderful God is! First, the possession of that great property gave work to the young men called of God to remain in the College for intercession. They were occupied all those years in felling timber on the estate and, as a consequence, were exempted from other service.

Then, while the war was still in progress, Mr. Howells was led to have plans drawn out for the building of houses on the estate. It was a providential guidance, because some time later the Government introduced a law whereby all land was made subject to charges in the event of development. A clause, however, was inserted in the Bill exempting any land for which plans had been passed before a certain date. Very few could take advantage of this, but the Penllergaer estate was one, and as a result many pounds were saved for God's Treasury.

The Penllergaer mansion was then offered to Dr. Barnardo's as a free gift to house war orphans. After long deliberations, however, the Council decided that the conversion, repairs and maintenance of the mansion would prove too expensive. The Glamorgan County Council then took it over as a school for backward children. But the estate around remained in the hands of the College, to bring back in due course the sum of money God had promised His servant it would produce for the Kingdom.

Through the years of war the Jews were never forgotten, although prayer to God was mainly for affairs of the nations. For, as Mr. Howells said, "When the war came, He changed us from praying regarding the Jews to the Beast [a name he commonly gave to the devil in the Nazi system], and said, 'Get victory over him.' " But it was after the war, in October and November 1947, that whole days were again given to praying through for the Jews' return to Palestine.

Mr. Howells recalled, "We pleaded that because of His covenant with Abraham 4,000 years ago, God would take His people back to their land, and Palestine should again become a Jewish State." The challenge that came before the College was: if the Jewish people did not go back after the 1914–18 war, would they go back after this one? They saw the hand of God in the setting up of a United Nations Committee to consider the question of Palestine. There was thanksgiving when the news was published that Britain was going to evacuate the country.

On eleven different days during those two months, prayer was concentrated on the coming United Nations vote. It was touch and go. On the day of voting, November 27, 1947, there was much prayer, but the news came that the partitioning of Palestine had not been carried. The College went back to yet more intense prayer, during which they saw in faith "God's angels influencing those men in the United Nations Conference in New York to work on behalf of God's people," and had full assurance of victory.

When, next day, the news came that the United Nations had passed the partitioning of Palestine by 33 votes to 13, and that the State of Israel was a fact, the College acclaimed it with rejoicing as "one of the greatest days for the Holy Ghost in the history of these 2,000 years. During all those centuries there wasn't a single sign that the country was to be given back to the Jews who were scattered all over the earth, but now, 4,000 years after His covenant with Abraham, He has gathered all the nations together and made them give much of the land of Palestine back to them."

One unusual ray of light was also given to Mr. Howells at that time concerning the Arabs. He said: "God put me aside for some days to reveal the position of the Arabs. In Genesis 16:12, God says of Ishmael that 'he shall dwell in the presence of all his brethren.' This is the problem. Does God mean the Arabs to dwell with the Jews? Abraham loved Ishmael and wanted him to have the inheritance; and God, who means what He says, declared: 'I have blessed him.' The Arabs only worship the One God. Did God mean them to be blessed as well as the Jews? They will afford shelter to the Jews (Isaiah 21: 13–15), and will be the first to come to Jerusalem to pay homage to the King (Isaiah 60:7).

"Just as we were only burdened for the Jews when we had to make intercession for them, so the Lord wanted us to have a concern for the Arabs also. They also are the sons of Abraham. Can the Holy Ghost bring in something which will break down the barrier between the Jews and Arabs that there may be a home and a blessing for both? Certainly the Arabs are the people of God, if they are to shield the Jews and live in those countries which are to escape out of the hand of the Beast."

34

Intercession for Dunkirk

During the four years previous to the outbreak of World War II, as we have already seen, the Lord was changing the burden on Rees Howells from local concerns—centering on the development of the College—to national and international affairs. As he said, "The world became our parish and we were led to be responsible to intercede for countries and nations." We have also seen how the Lord was preparing, in the company at the College, a special instrument of intercession for the coming world crisis.

It was in March 1936 that Mr. Howells began to see clearly that Hitler was Satan's agent for preventing the gospel going to every creature. As he said later, "In fighting Hitler we have always said that we were not up against man but the devil. Mussolini is a man, but Hitler is different. He can tell the day this 'spirit' came into him." For several years Mr. Howells stressed the fact that God must destroy him if the vision of the gospel to every creature was to be fulfilled.

At first he believed that God would prevent war altogether. We have seen how the College fought through on their knees during the Munich crisis and how they believed for peace. As the clouds over Europe grew darker, Mr. Howells still believed that God would intervene and prevent war. He stood to his prediction right up to the day of the declaration of war between Britain and Germany on September 3, 1939. Even then he was not moved.

Although people said that the prediction was wrong, he thanked God he had made it. "If I had a choice again about making this prediction," he said, "I would make it tonight, although it has gone much farther than we thought it would. Hitler must be put out of the way because, if he isn't, he will come up again in another two years. I want to know that the Holy Spirit is stronger than the devil in the Nazi system. This is the battle of the ages, and victory here means victory for millions of people."

On the day of the declaration of war, he published the following statement: "The Lord has made known to us that He is going to destroy Hitler and the Nazi regime, that the world may know that it was God and God alone who has scattered the dictators. Three and a half years ago the College prayed this prayer for weeks and months and we firmly believe He will now answer it.

"God has isolated Germany so that He may get at this evil system, which is the Antichrist, and release Germany, the land of the Reformation. He will deal with the Nazis as He dealt with the Egyptian army in the time of Moses. God will cause Hitler to fall on the battlefield or by a mutiny or a great rising in Germany against the Nazis." So, far from the declaration of war shaking him and those with him, it only sent them, more determined than ever, to their knees.

They were now called in a new way to pay the vow they had made three years before—to give their lives over "to fight the battles of the Kingdom, as really as if called to fight on the Western Front." This stand of faith against war in order that the gospel might not be hindered was proved to be God's way of placing upon that company a responsibility from which they could never come free until the enemy that God was dealing with should be destroyed.

When, after a month of hostilities, an offer of peace was made by Hitler, the College stood with the Prime Minister in stating that war must be continued, "until Hitlerism is overthrown," even though, like so many more, the College had much to lose by its continuance.

The conviction of the College was expressed in the title of a book which Mr. Howells wrote in the opening weeks of the war and which was published in December 1939, called *God Challenges the Dictators—Doom of Nazis Predicted.* In it he said, "The God of Daniel will deliver Pastor Niemoller and the hundreds of other German Evangelicals who have followed him to the concentration camps . . . . Their places will one day be occupied by the fanatical Nazi leaders, if any of them escape a speedy death."

After an indictment of Mussolini he stated, "When victory over Germany comes . . . Ethiopia should also be given back to the Ethiopians, and this may also be in God's divine plan to evangelize Ethiopia." He also declared that "Bolshevism and Soviet Russia are being used in the plan of God to break the evil Nazi regime." But of Stalin he predicted, "The devil has used, and may yet use, this man to be the greatest foe to the Church that the world has ever known."

Although his confidence was that God would intervene to deal with the enemy, he wrote, "We may have many a setback before He does so . . . . It may be that we, like the Israelites [referring to Judges 20], will have to cry out to God in our extremity for the help which will certainly come." It is truly remarkable to look back now and realize that these things were in print before the end of 1939.

Shortly after this Mr. Howells made a further prediction which was published by *The Western Mail* on January 8, 1940, under a headline of "Welsh Bible College Director Urges Prayer to Stop War." It quoted him as saying: "If all the righteous in the country will send up effectual prayer, we feel sure that we shall prevail and open Penllergaer on Whitmonday without war or blackout . . . . What a relief to millions of people if God will intervene and bring the war to an end by Whitsuntide."

Little did he imagine when that prediction was made that the days around that Whitsunday, May 12, were to be the darkest in the history of his nation and the nearest that Britain had come in nearly 400 years to the invasion of her shores. It was on May 10 that Hitler's armored columns broke in on Holland and Belgium, and May 29 was that never-to-be-forgotten date in British history, the Dunkirk evacuation, to be followed shortly after by Mr. Churchill's memorable call to "blood and sweat and toil and tears."

In spite of this apparent setback, as we read the diaries of the daily College meetings (three meetings on most days) we find ourselves among certainly not a fearful company—nor even chiefly among a praying one—but rather among those who are already on victory ground when all around men's hearts are failing them for fear. And what gave them such clarity and assurance that theirs was the victory? The outward "death" of the prediction!

If we say God was not with them, we may well ask ourselves this question: "Was there anywhere else in the whole of Britain, or America, or elsewhere among God's people another such company, maybe a hundred strong, who were on their knees day by day holding fast the victory by faith while soldiers across the water were retreating mile by mile, whole countries surrendering, and the enemy within sight of their goal?"

From this time on, through all the years of the war the whole College was in prayer every evening from seven o'clock to midnight with only a brief interval for supper. They never missed a day. This was in addition to an hour's prayer meeting every morning, and very often at midday. There were many special periods when every day was given up wholly to prayer and fasting.

In the meetings just before Whitsunday Mr. Howells said: "Through God we made the prediction; through God we stand to it; and through God we are going against the enemy. He tells me tonight, 'Don't you fear because of that prediction you sent out; don't you fear the Nazis.' I think what a glory it is that we don't need to change our prayers one bit, in spite of the present developments. I am so glad that it has been the Kingdom we have had before us all the time in the last nine months, and I haven't a single regret. The Lord has said, 'I am going to deal with the Nazis.' It has been a battle between the Holy Spirit and the devil which we have been fighting for four years."

On Whitsunday, when, instead of peace having been declared, Hitler only two days before had invaded Holland and Belgium, Rees Howells said to the College meeting: "We shall never defend the prediction. The point is, Can God put a doubt in us who have really believed? If God tells you that this delay is for His glory, then you must take victory in it. There is no glory in delay, unless there was faith to put it through. I would be a different man today if there was failure, but the Holy Spirit is not a failure. I can really thank Him for the delay. I wouldn't be without this experience for the world. Very strange that what is death in the eyes of the world is victory to the Holy Ghost."

The next day he said, "We could never have had a greater death than in this prediction being delayed. But we are not going to have resurrection on one point more than has gone to the cross. I preached victory yesterday without a visible victory. There is a death in every grade, but as really as you die, there will be fruit to a hundredfold.

"We are going up to the battle, and I am sure of victory as of the dawn. If you know you have faith for something, would you not go on until you got it? I would like this to ring out to the world: 'The Lord, He is the God!' "

As the Nazis poured through Europe, the College stood daily before God. We quote from notes taken of Mr. Howells' messages in the meetings:

May 16, 9:30 a.m. The day after Holland had surrendered: "Today is probably the greatest battle in history. Can God do something today? Now when the Germans say, 'We have got the Allies on the run,' can God do it? Keep your eyes on God today and get this victory."

2 p.m. "The Lord has made very plain that the victory is from Him and no one else, and He is to have all the glory. God gets at the enemy visibly and invisibly, through the army and through us."

5:30 p.m. "The position is most serious in France, but even if the French and British are fighting against such great odds, the Lord is able to help them."

May 17, 9:30 a.m. "God will not do a bit more through you than you have faith for. The victory last night was in seeing that no matter how near the enemy came, the Holy Ghost is stronger than he. You are more responsible for this victory to-day than those men on the battlefield. You must be dead to everything else but this fight."

1 p.m. "Because you have committed yourselves, you are responsible. You will never have peace again until the world has peace, but you have a place in the cleft of the Rock."

3:30 p.m. "We are here until these Nazis are put out."

7 p.m. "If the Lord finds us quite willing in this death-life, and that we have got victory in the test, will He allow us to prevail upon Him now to finish it? If we believed last Saturday, we are believing tonight. I am not willing that thousands of our boys should be lost, because there has to be the 'doom of the Nazis,' and it will come now if we can prevail. If this had been a failure, God would have been against us, but He shows He is pleased with us."

May 18, 9:30 a.m. "Unless God intervenes today in a miraculous way, I believe we have lost. I would be willing to die, but I cannot afford to die, neither can we afford that Hitler should live."

2:30 p.m. "I want to fight with this enemy again this weekend as if it were the end of civilization. You don't leave anything to chance in this. Don't allow those young men at the Front to do more than you do here. I do ask Him to bring a real disaster to the Nazis this weekend."

6:30 p.m. "As the Lord gave us the prediction, and we have had victory in it, and the delay has not changed our faith a bit, then we must come back and ask Him when He is going to do it. I feel tonight that whatever these Nazis do, they cannot escape the Holy Spirit. Christianity is quite safe. If you have faith, you can leave it in His hand, and He will intervene in the right time. We can't inquire when He is going to do it if we haven't got faith for Him to do it."

9:30 p.m. "It is not you struggling, but God doing, and you coming to know what God is doing. Is it God who has drawn Hitler across that line with his 2,500 armored cars? I want the Lord to discomfit this man and those armored cars."

May 19, 9:30 a.m. "These Nazis will not destroy civilization. When they get near enough, God will deal with them. When the Holy Spirit has gone to the victory side, you could never convince the man or woman who has gone to the victory side with Him that He is a failure."

9:15 p.m. "Now is the best time to test the Bible in wars, because we are in one ourselves."

May 20, 9 a.m. "The next 24 hours will be the crisis in this great battle. They are ready to take our country at any moment. Even before lunchtime the history of the world may be changed. Such a thing as this has not happened to us before, and you do not know how much faith is needed. We are coming to the Lord this morning and telling Him our eyes are on Him today. Unless He intervenes, we are lost. I don't doubt the Lord for one second, but I must be very careful."

2:30 p.m. "I think tonight of sending the book *God Challenges the Dictators* to Mr. Churchill to encourage him at this moment. The army is losing ground every day. In the book it has been said that man would not be able to end this, but that God has said, 'Don't expect Me to do it until you get to your extremity.' The only thing we want the Lord to make plain to us is, Are we up to the place He wants us to be at this moment? The only thing I want is not to doubt in the time of crisis—and it is going to be a real crisis."

7 p.m. "Today I have sent the book to Mr. Chamberlain, Lord Halifax and Mr. Churchill—in the darkest hour."

May 21, 9 a.m. Fear of invasion: "Yesterday was the darkest day in the history of this country, especially after the Prime Minister's speech. Everyone in town is expecting the enemy to invade this country. We have told the Lord, 'Our lives for victory.' We ought to pray now for the Lord to stop them coming over to this country."

2:30 p.m. "We must pray for the Lord to keep the enemy in check. He is like a roaring lion."

7 p.m. "The French Premier says tonight, 'It is only a miracle that will save us.' The test is, whether the Bible is true. I am willing to risk my life to prove it, and I want to tell you tonight that it is quite true. See that your believing is right, and if it is, you don't need to have any fear."

May 22, 9 a.m. "The world is in a panic today, and certainly we would be too unless we were quite sure the Lord had spoken to us. The destiny of England will be at stake today and tomorrow."

2:30 p.m. "In a battle such as we are in today, you cannot trust in a meeting or in feelings. We must go back to what God has told us. There is an enemy that we must keep in check until God does the big thing."

From the night of May 22 to 25 Mr. Howells no longer came to the meetings; other members of the staff took them. He went away alone with God to battle through, and, as others have testified, the crushing burden of those days broke his body. He literally laid down his life.

May 26 was the day of public prayer in Britain. Mr. Churchill said of the May 26 Service of Intercession in Westminster Abbey: "The English are loath to expose their feelings, but in my stall in the choir I could feel the pent-up passionate emotion, and also the fear of the congregation—not of death or wounds or national loss, but of defeat and the final ruin of Britain."

May 26, 9:30 a.m. Mr. Howells returned to the College meetings and said: "All you can do today when a cry will go up from the country is to be in a position to take the answer from God. The question this morning is, Can we take the answer? If you ever cried, you ought to cry today."

11:15 a.m. "How can you be sure that the Nazis will not take our country? All the leading people know today that unless God intervenes, we will be slaves. We prayed for Ethiopia and other countries, so our cry is not a selfish one."

2:30 p.m. "We are going against this Beast as David went against Goliath."

May 27, 9 a.m. "There is intercession and faith, so the Lord can do a mighty deed. Our people will see God answering their prayers and they will have all the joy of it."

2:45 p.m. "It is as much as I can do to believe today. The news between the two meetings was awful—hell upon earth."

On May 28 Mr. Howells again was alone with God. In the meetings, the prayer was for God to intervene at Dunkirk and save the men. As the Spirit came upon them in prayer and supplication, what one prayed at the end expressed the assurance given to all: "I feel sure something has happened."

May 29 was the day of the evacuation of Dunkirk. Mr. Howells said, "Let us be clear in our prayer that the intercession is gained. The battle is the Holy Spirit's. See Him outside yourselves tonight; He is there on the battlefield with His drawn sword."

May 30, 7:30 p.m. "From a worldly standpoint there is no hope of victory; but God has said it. I could not come tonight and ask Him to intervene because we have already said that He is going to intervene. Instead of bad news about our soldiers, if He is on the field of battle He can change that and make it very good news. Oh, for God to lift us up tonight! We are not to run into any panic thinking the Nazis are going to win: Germany must be delivered as well as England and France. We may have to go through far greater sufferings yet, but I am not going to doubt the final issue. We state in plainest terms: *The enemy will not invade Christian England.*"

When we look back now after these years, many in Britain still recall the terror of those days. Remembering the miracle of Dunkirk, acknowledged by various leaders to be an intervention from God—the calm sea allowing the smallest boats to cross, the almost complete evacuation of English troops—and then the lead Mr. Churchill gave to the nation, how thankful we are that God had this company of hidden intercessors whose lives were on the altar day after day as they stood in the gap for the deliverance of Britain.

35

The Battle of Britain

The next battle of intercession was over the air raids and the crisis of the "Battle of Britain," when Goering made his great attempt to gain mastery of the air in preparation for the invasion of England. In each of these vital matters, nothing was left to chance or a "shot-in-the-dark" type of praying. Everything was examined in God's presence and motives were sifted until the Holy Spirit could show His servant intelligently that there was an undeniable claim for prayer to be answered. Then faith would stand to the claim and lay hold of the victory; and there would be no rest until he had God's own assurance that faith had prevailed and victory was certain. It was not just praying and then *hoping* for the answer. We quote from notes taken in the meetings at that time.

On September 2, 1940, Mr. Howells said: "I want to see if we have a claim to be free from care when these planes are around. We ran to stand in the breach to save the Jewish children from Hitler when he was throwing them out. Can we now claim protection for all the missionaries' children? Unless my faith is equal to the occasion for protection I should bring every one of the children up to the shelter tonight, and I would be there with them. Must we have fear because others have fear? If I trusted God to bring these properties into being, I am going to trust God to protect them. I want you to get a foundation for this trust. We need a real foundation for our faith, in case the raids will last for months. Can we trust Him for the impossible in this, the same as in finance?

"The only thing I am afraid of is that I should miss God's will. Many people are afraid of consequences. I must be clear on this point, for God says, 'If it is the *consequences* you are afraid of, don't come to Me for protection.' There is a great difference between a selfish fear of consequences and wanting God's protection because you have a work to carry out for Him. Have you really got victory?"

Mr. Howells' mention of the shelter to which he said he could take the children referred to his obligation to provide a shelter for the day scholars, then numbering about 300. But for the other scholars and the missionaries' children, numbering about 60 (who were part of the College family), the Lord had told him to provide neither shelters nor gas masks (although any individual was perfectly free to have one if he should wish). God fully vindicated his stand throughout the war by not allowing a single bomb to fall on any College property, although the town, with its strategic docks, had some very heavy raids. But to continue from the journals:

September 3. After a heavy raid in the night: "I am sure the Lord took me up town to see about £2,000,000 worth of property on the ground. I thought, 'Was it worth taking Penllergaer, if this is what happens? Is it worth carrying a burden and agonizing for the sake of the Kingdom?' I saw what these properties will be like unless God protects them. I found myself praying for the town as much as I had prayed for the College the night before."

September 4. "The situation in the country because of air raids may become very serious. We have never walked this way before. The important thing is to find out where God is in this. When you are in danger every night, it takes you a long time to be sure that you are under God's protection. Can you say you are safe in the air raids? Has God told you? You may try to use the Word of God without having His power behind it. If God is going to deliver from this hell, there will have to be some power released. Unless you are sure of your own victory, you will never be able to pray for the deliverance of the country. We have bound the devil over and over again, and I hope we shall do it again when God's time comes in this war."

September 7. "How many people have been moved by the affliction of these air raids? If you can believe that you have been delivered from hell, why can't you believe that you have been delivered from air raids? I have always found something that has given me joy all day long and my joy today is that we have God's protection. But unless we are really trusting Him, where does the praise come in? This peace the Savior gives is not an artificial one. It is so deep that even the devil can't disturb it. You can't hear things in the Spirit while you have any turmoil or fear in you. You can't take a shade of fear into the presence of God."

September 8, 9 a.m. National Day of Prayer. "Our country has only the outward form of religion, neither cold nor hot, like the church at Laodicea. May God bring the nation back. Our one cause for praise is that the enemy has not been able to invade our country."

At the midday service, just as Mr. Howells began to speak, the Nazi planes passed overhead. The guns in the field below crashed out and the siren sounded but he went on with his message and "the congregation was held spellbound."

It was at this point that the burden of prayer for protection and the questionings of the past few days changed into praise and certainty. Full assurance of victory was given, and it rings out in Rees Howells' words: "What victory! Those who are in the Spirit see it as victory, because He has found believing in us. What joy! What praise! God would probably not give faith for victory in the war until personal victory was first gained." The all-clear sounded as the service finished. They sang in closing: "Death is vanquished, tell it with joy, ye faithful."

In the afternoon meeting of the same day, he said: "I could now put it in print that no devil can touch anyone here. There is no need to pray any more. When you believe, you finish with prayer. We have never been in such victory before, carrying on exactly as if there was no war. How could we get victory for the world unless we had first believed it for ourselves? You can't trust in anything except believing prayer. How the Holy Ghost came down this morning in the communion service and told us of His victory!"

September 9. "The Holy Ghost has found faith equal to what He wants to do. Take care you are believing. Believing is the most delicate thing you can think of. It is like a vapor; you can easily miss it. The victory happened yesterday morning, and if you didn't see it you may never see it. From this time on He can guide this battle, but He couldn't do it before without faith."

September 10. "What if millions of prayers went up on the Day of Prayer and no one had believed? After the victory of Sunday there is great liberty to pray that God will really deal with the devil in the Nazis and put an end to this wicked system. Our prayer for London is that God will turn the tide now and save life. No doubt the enemy is pouring scorn on last Sunday's National Day of Prayer."

September 11, with the Battle of Britain over London and the south of England at its fiercest: "There have been so many places bombed in London, even Buckingham Palace has been touched. I was burdened to pray for the King and Queen, and I believe our prayer will be answered. I am just watching how God will take hold of the enemy."

September 12. "We prayed last night that London would be defended and that the enemy would fail to break through, and God answered prayer. Unless God can get hold of this devil and bind him, no man is safe. If we have protection for our properties, why not get protection for the country? What wonderful days these are."

September 14. "Because we have believed, God has made known to us what is to come to pass. Every creature is to hear the gospel; Palestine is to be regained by the Jews; and the Savior is to return."

Mr. Churchill, in his *War Memoirs*, gives September 15 as "the culminating date" in that Battle of the Air. He tells how he visited the Operations Room of the R.A.F. that day and watched as the enemy squadrons poured over and his own countrymen went up to meet them. The moment came when he finally asked the Air Marshal, "What other reserves have we?" "There are none," he answered, and reported afterwards how grave Mr. Churchill had looked. "And well I might," added the Prime Minister. Then another five minutes passed, and "it appeared that the enemy were going home. The shifting of the discs on the table showed a continuous eastward movement of German bombers and fighters. No new attack appeared. In another ten minutes the action was ended."

There seemed no reason why the *Luftwaffe* should have turned for home just at the moment when victory was in their grasp. But we know why.

After the war, Air Chief Marshal Lord Dowding, Commander-in-Chief of Fighter Command in the Battle of Britain, made this revealing observation: "Even during the battle one realized from day to day how much external support was coming in. At the end of the battle one had the sort of feeling that there had been some special Divine intervention to alter some sequence of events which would otherwise have occurred."

36

Russia, North Africa, Italy, "D" Day

Victory in the Battle of Britain saved the country from invasion, but the enemy sought to recompense himself by heavier, indiscriminate night bombing, which continued into 1941. In January of that year this constant bombing of Britain became a prayer burden at the College until it reached a crisis.

"I feel much more strongly today," said Mr. Howells in the January 20 meeting, "that God has stopped me from praying more for this town than for the country. He tells me, 'If these air raids are going to be repeated, I cannot guarantee you will be safe, so come and pray them out of the country.' And I said to Him, 'You protect us now, until we get a chance to come up and believe You.' "

Ten days were spent in prayer, and then on January 28 the journal stated: "Believed for the protection of the country." This was followed by the remarkable petition: "Lord, turn the enemy down to the Mediterranean," and thus relieve the pressure on Britain by turning Hitler's attention in another direction. Just over two months later, on April 6, war was declared by Hitler on Yugoslavia and Greece, and this was followed by the invasion of Crete and North Africa. With these new commitments the enemy was obliged to turn from the destruction of Britain, and so the immediate crisis for Britain passed over.

The next prayer was greater still. We suppose nothing gave the world a bigger shock through the whole course of the war than when, without a word of warning, Hitler swung around and invaded Russia. If anything was seen to be an intervention of God to help the Allies, it was that. The secular papers spoke of it in the words of the pagan proverb: "Whom the gods would destroy they first make mad." That decision of Hitler was reckoned as one of the great acts of divine intervention which spelled the "doom of the Nazis."

The invasion of Russia started at 4 a.m. on June 22, 1941. But seven weeks prior, on May 2, God had begun to speak to Mr. Howells about Russia. He had said that day, "Much as we long to see the war finished, it seems that God is saying, 'There is one country more I want to bring judgment on, and that is Communist Russia.' "

And again on the next day: "Russia comes before me. Is it right for Stalin and his followers to escape? If God gives us the choice, would we tell Him to prolong the war, although we are losing on every point?" And again: "We ask the Lord to weaken Russia and Japan, even if it means prolonging the war for five years. Can't the Lord turn the enemy's drive into Russia? If God does not deal with Russia now, He will have to make another war to do so. I say He ought to bring Russia into it, no matter how long it will take, unless He has another way to get at these communists."

From that time this became the main prayer of the College: "Lord, bring Russia into the war and deal with Communism." Six weeks later Russia had come in! But very soon the danger was of another kind. Russia was in, but after a few short weeks was facing imminent collapse. As the German hordes poured into that country, how well we remember the anxiety with which the free world watched the gradual disintegration of the Russian armies, and the constantly closer approach of the Nazis to Moscow.

It was a race with winter. It was a repetition of the famous invasion of Napoleon. Hitler proclaimed that he would succeed where Napoleon had failed and winter in an intact Moscow. Would he? Did anybody in those tense days believe he would not?

Hitler's armies were almost at the gates of the city. On Sunday, October 19, 1941, Mrs. Howells relates that very early that morning Mr. Howells told her he would go down and hear the seven o'clock news to see if Moscow had fallen. When he came back, he reported it had not fallen, but that they were expecting bad news any time.

A few minutes after that, the Lord began to speak to him: "Is there any need for Moscow to fall? Why don't you pray and believe for Me to save Moscow and give a setback to the Nazis?"

Dr. Kenneth G. Symonds, F.R.C.S., who was a member of the College staff for a number of years, tells us of the meeting that Sunday morning. "The Director opened his message by saying that the first thing the Lord had told him that morning was, 'Pray that Moscow will not fall!' It seemed ridiculously impossible, for we had heard that its fall was inevitable.

"But although the prayer was so far beyond us, yet the Spirit laid it on us. It seemed that He prayed in spite of us, so we travailed all day until late in the meeting that night when He so inspired us through His servant that we had the assurance that God was answering. The Lord gave liberty to pray that the Nazis might be utterly overthrown in a Russian winter. We shall never forget the joy of victory He gave us as faith mounted up during those days."

The second day the news was that the Russians had taken fresh courage and the snow was falling heavily in some parts. Four days later in the meeting Mr. Howells said, "I say now, 'Thus saith the Lord: he [Hitler] is wintering in the Russian snows.' " We all know the end of the story: Moscow never fell, and Goering, recounting later the misfortunes of that winter, stated that three million of the flower of the Nazi army perished in the snow. Victor Kravchenko, in his book *I Chose Freedom*, said: "The Germans could have taken Moscow those days virtually without a struggle. . . . Why they turned back is a mystery only the Germans themselves can solve for history."

God now began to turn the prayers of the College in yet another direction. With the Nazis marching through Yugoslavia and Greece and capturing Crete, and with the menace of

Rommel and the Italians growing in North Africa, prayer began to be centered on the Bible Lands.

This was really one of the main burdens of prayer at the College because, long before, God had revealed to them that this was not just a European war, but that through it "in the determinate counsel and foreknowledge of God" the Jews would return to Palestine, the gospel go out to every creature, and the Savior be able to return. Thus as soon as the Bible Lands seemed in danger of invasion, God turned their prayer in that direction. "I am sure," said Mr. Howells, "the enemy will never touch Palestine, Syria and Iraq."

The area of greatest immediate danger was North Africa. With the appearance of Rommel and the German armored divisions there, the menace to Egypt became grave; and if Egypt fell, the door was wide open to Palestine. Again we remember those dark days when Rommel had driven back our armies and was almost knocking on the gates of Alexandria.

"Unless God will intervene on behalf of Palestine," said Mr. Howells on July 4, 1942, "there will be no safety there for the Jews. These Bible Lands must be protected, because it is to these lands the Savior will come back. If I had the choice today, I would say to God, 'Take all I have, but preserve Palestine.' We want to say to God today, 'Unless there is a special reason for Egypt to fall, don't let Alexandria be taken, but give Rommel a setback.' Can I carry the same burden today for Alexandria as I would if Swansea were being attacked?"

It was a Saturday, and there were not usually prayer meetings on Saturday afternoons; but that day the College was called to spend the afternoon in prayer for God to save Alexandria and turn the tide in North Africa. There was a heavy burden, but very great liberty in prayer. In the meeting that evening Mr. Howells said, "Is this prayer we prayed this afternoon of the Holy Ghost, that the enemy is *not* to take Alexandria? I am speaking to all of you who took a real part in the prayers against the enemy, praying him down to the Mediterranean, praying him to Russia, keeping him out of Moscow! Is this prayer of the Holy Spirit? If it is, we can be as sure of the enemy not taking Alexandria as the people will be when they hear it."

Then on July 5: "All I want to know is, Has the intercession been gained for the Bible Lands? If it has, we have the right to prevail on God that the enemy is not to take Alexandria. The first test point since Moscow is Alexandria."

That evening Mr. Howells and the College came through to victory. "I thought he might be allowed to take Egypt," he said, "but I know now he will never take Egypt—neither Alexandria nor Cairo will fall." And at the end of the meeting he declared, "I have been stirred to my depths today. I have been like a man ploughing his way through sand. But now I am on top of it; now I am gripping it. I am handling it; I can shake it."

The following week they read in the news how grave things had been in North Africa on that very Saturday when the extra prayer meeting was called, and it was over that weekend that the tide turned at El Alamein, saving Alexandria. Major P. W. Rainer, who was responsible for supplying the Eighth Army with water, tells this story of a remarkable and possibly deciding incident in the battle for Alexandria in his book, *Pipe Line to Battle*, as quoted in the magazine of the Merchant Service Officers' Christian Association of April 1944.

Between Rommel's men and Alexandria were the remnants of a British army—fifty tanks, a few score field guns, and about 5,000 soldiers. The sides were equally matched, with the Germans holding the advantage, because of their superior 88 mm. guns. Both armies were near exhaustion from heat, dust and lack of water. The battle was grim. In the words of Major Rainer: "The sun was almost overhead, and our men were fast reaching the end of their endurance, when the Nazis broke. Ten minutes more and it might have been us.

"Slowly, sullenly the Mark IV tanks lumbered back from their battle smoke. And then an incredible thing happened: 1,100 men of the 90th Light Panzer Division, the elite of the Afrika Korps, came stumbling across the barren sand with their hands in the air. Cracked and black with coagulated blood, their swollen tongues were protruding from their mouths. Crazily they tore water bottles from the necks of our men and poured life-giving swallows between their parched lips."

Major Rainer then goes on to give this reason for their surrender. The Germans had been twenty-four hours without water when they overran the British defences and found a 6-inch water pipe. They shot holes in it and drank deeply. Only when they had taken great gulps did they realize that it was *sea* water!

The pipe had only just been laid and Major Rainer had started to test it. Fresh water, however, was never used for tests on pipes—it was too precious. "Two days later it would have been full of fresh water. . . . The Nazis didn't detect the salt at once, because their sense of taste had already been anesthetized by the brackish water they had been used to, and by thirst."

The surrender of those 1,100 crack soldiers may have been the deciding incident in the battle for Alexandria. The editor's comment is: "Such an incredible happening as this cannot be treated as a mere coincidence. Assuredly the hand of Almighty God is in evidence once more, coming to our aid when weighty issues are in the balance."

The attention of the College then had to be turned again to the Russian campaign, if the Bible Lands were to be safe. The danger from the south was now over, but as the Germans, having failed in their attempt on Moscow, pressed eastward through southern Russia and approached Stalingrad, they were coming near the Caucasus Mountains. Once across that range, the door would be wide open to the Bible Lands from the north.

Dr. Symonds tells us that "The Nazis had already penetrated the defences of Stalingrad and were fighting in the suburbs of the town, when the Holy Spirit was urging him to pray that Stalingrad should not fall. The reason was that Stalingrad is the gateway to the Caucasus, and the Caucasus to the Bible Lands.

"The enemy had made two attempts to occupy these lands, the first via Crete, which brought the prayer from the Spirit that the Nazi hordes should be turned against Russia; and the second via North Africa, which had resulted in the divine intervention in answer to believing prayer at El Alamein. But this prayer for Stalingrad seemed the hardest of all to take hold of. For a whole fortnight we wrestled, the Spirit through His servant insisting that, the prayer having come from Him, we were to be responsible to see it through to a successful issue, as with Moscow.

"In spite of our cries, the enemy continued to advance until half of the city was in his hands. The fighting there from house to house was some of the most desperate in the whole war; but the conflict in the Spirit was correspondingly desperate. Contrary to all human reason, as the news got darker, faith rose higher, until we found the enemy was giving way before us. At the same time the tide turned in the visible battle and, to the wonder of the world, the Nazi army was driven out again utterly broken and demoralized. It was another mighty triumph of the Holy Spirit."

Some months later, with these four great prayer battles behind them—the invasions of Britain, Alexandria, Moscow and Stalingrad—the College personnel were much interested to see an article published in the press by the military commentator General J. R. C. Fuller, in which he gave four reasons for the impending doom of the Nazis. "Hitler's four blunders," he called them. Blunder No. 1 was missing the chance to invade Britain. Blunder No. 2, his failure to attack Egypt and gain Alexandria. Blunder No. 3, "Everything in the Russian campaign depended on the fall of Moscow. Yet Hitler turned away to other objectives." Blunder No. 4, "Hitler's final mistake —the great attack on Stalingrad."

On two further occasions there were times of special concentration in prayer—one in the invasion of Italy, and the other for "D" Day. In the battle for Italy the danger spot was Salerno, where Allied troops landed in September 1943, to capture some strategic heights and open the way for the invading forces from the south to reach Rome.

"The day of the landing at Salerno and its sequel will always be outstanding in my memory," says Dr. Symonds. "We had the first evening prayer meeting as usual in the Conference Hall, and gathered again at 9:45 p.m. for the late meeting in Derwen Fawr. It had a solemn tone from the outset, the Director's voice trembling with the burden of his message, and scarcely audible as he said, 'The Lord has burdened me between the meetings with the invasion at Salerno. I believe our men are in great difficulties, and the Lord has told me that unless we can pray through, they are in danger of losing their hold.'

"The awe of God settled down upon us, for this came as a complete surprise. There had been no official news to this effect on the wireless, and we ourselves had previously had some rejoicing that Italy was at last on the point of being delivered from the Fascist and Nazi tyranny. Before long we were on our knees crying to God for Him to intervene. The Spirit took hold of us and suddenly broke right through in the prayers, and we found ourselves praising and rejoicing, believing that God had heard and answered.

"We could not go on praying any longer, so we rose from our knees and began to sing praises, the Spirit witnessing in all our hearts that God had wrought some miraculous intervention in Italy. The victory was so outstanding that I looked at the clock as we rose to sing. It was on the stroke of 11 p.m.

"We waited to hear the midnight news. The announcer gravely told us in effect exactly what the Director had told us from the Lord—that unless some miracle happened, our troops were in grave danger of losing the beachhead before the morning. This only served to confirm to us the guidance of the Spirit, and we felt more confident than ever that the victory was certain.

"The news the next morning was more hopeful, but we eagerly awaited newspaper reports from the Front. We were not disappointed. On Thursday morning one of the daily newspapers displayed a front page headline in large print, 'The

Miracle of Salerno.' The account of the reporter personally at the Front ran somewhat as follows: 'I was with our advanced troops in the invasion of Salerno on Monday. The enemy artillery was advancing rapidly and with ceaseless firing. The noise was terrible, and it was obvious that unless a miracle happened, our troops could never hold up the advance long enough for the beachhead to be established.

" 'Suddenly for no accountable reason the firing ceased and the Nazi artillery stopped its advance. A deathly stillness settled on the scene. We waited in breathless anticipation, but nothing happened. I looked at my watch—*it was eleven o'clock at night.* Still we waited, but still nothing happened; and nothing happened all that night, but those hours made all the difference to the invasion. By the morning the beachhead was established.' "

In the last great prayer-battle of the war—for the opening of the Second Front—we will quote again some of Mr. Howells' own words. On April 6, 1944, just two months before "D" Day, he was saying in the meetings: "We are concerned for the young people who are about to enter the Second Front. Can we believe that our young men can go through with the minimum of loss? If God intervened in Moscow, Stalingrad, Alexandria and our own country, can't He intervene in the Second Front and stop us from having a setback?

"We have a perfect right to ask God to come and fight with our young men, because our leaders only want the Atlantic Charter and its Four Freedoms as the result of this war. If we got victory at Stalingrad, we can get it here. We know that He is on the side of our men, and I see nothing tonight but victory."

A month later (May 7), he said: "I am speaking at a time when 5,000,000 men are facing the Second Front. These young men from America are in our country waiting for the invasion, and many thousands may be lost. In Verdun the French lost 1,000,000. If I am not called up to fight, and I know another way to help them and I don't do it, I ought to be killed instead of them. They are facing death, and anyone who has faced death knows it is a serious thing, and they are facing it for you and me. If they suffer more than we suffer for them, it will be our lifelong shame.

"If there is a Second Front next week, is there a God in heaven who can intervene? When it starts, Governor Dewey of New York is calling all his State to prayer. The worst of it is that Germany is a Protestant country, and so are we, but it is not the German nation we are fighting: it is the Nazi regime. We believe God is on our side and He says, 'I will not sheathe the sword until the Charter is established and the world set free.' "

In another meeting God gave the assurance to the College that on "D" Day "He was going over before our troops, and they would not have a setback." "The believing was so strong that we were able to take it," wrote one who was present. "After the burden we had been carrying, the relief was so great that I went to my room, fell on my knees and burst into tears. They were tears of joy and sheer relief from a tremendous tension. It was just as real to me then as if the whole Second Front had been established and the victory actually won."

On June 6, the day of the opening of the Second Front, Mr. Howells read with great approval General Eisenhower's Order of the Day to the assault troops, in which he said, "The hopes and prayers of liberty-loving people everywhere march with you . . . . Let us beseech the blessing of Almighty God upon this great and noble undertaking"; and still more, the wonderful speech of the King, which he broadcast to the country, solemnly calling his people to prayer and dedication. "Surely not one of us is too busy to play our part in a nation-wide—perchance a worldwide—vigil of prayer as the great crusade sets forth."

In the meeting Mr. Howells said: "If there is going to be a Day of Prayer, it ought to be a day of victory and moving God." And in his own prayer at the end of that meeting, thinking of the assault troops already landing in Normandy, he prayed, "If You hadn't intervened at Dunkirk, not one of us would be here today. So lay a burden on us; don't allow us to be slack. If Hitler had won, Christianity, civilization and freedom would have gone. O Lord, protect and keep our men! Don't allow us to pray any differently from what we would if we were on the front line. We do believe the end of this will be victory."

Finally, on July 8, he said: "I don't think there is anything to compare with the night we invaded Normandy. We said that God was going before our men, and it wasn't going to be like Dunkirk. The *Daily Telegraph* reported that it was only that night the U-boats did not patrol the channel. The way we went over to Normandy was beyond imagination—4,000 ships and 11,000 planes—and they never met a single ship or plane of the enemy! God said, 'I am going over and there won't be a setback'; and, although while I am preaching there is a big battle on, I go back to His word that there will be no reverses."

The consummation of these six years of prayer came in June 1945 with the establishment of the United Nations at San Francisco. No vain hopes of final world peace were based on that, however, for the prayer in the College for the gospel to go to every creature and for the Jews to return to Palestine has always been with the one great anticipation of the return of the Savior in glory and the setting up of the Millennial Kingdom, when *at last* there will be "peace on earth." But the establishment of the United Nations was the answer to these years of prayer for the reopening of the world to the gospel, so that every creature might hear in this generation.

37

Home Call

This period of intercession was now ended. During the war years God had called the College apart to intercede for the world, as years before He had shut in Rees Howells alone with Himself to intercede for one soul. Now that the war was over, links of fellowship were renewed with the foreign field. The College has always stood for fellowship with all faithful servants of Christ throughout the world. Through the years students have gone out with various organizations, and numbers of mission societies have been helped financially. Leaders and members of many missions have been visitors at the College, and from the time it was founded, God told His servant never to let a missionary visit the place without sending him away with a gift—even if it was the last he had in his possession.

Now that the College was freed from the burden of prayer for the war, the Lord began to lay upon them afresh the needs of the mission field. The annual Every Creature Conference was started in 1947, and the training of students for all fields increased.

The special burden on Mr. Howells' own heart was finance for getting the gospel to every creature—finance which could be expended freely in the support of God's servants in all lands. This burden never left him till Sunday, January 15, 1950. In the nine o'clock meeting that night he read the songs of Moses and David; then he said, "Everything in me is praising God because the Holy Ghost can say, 'I have finished the work Thou gavest Me to do.' Every creature will hear the gospel, the finance for the Vision is safe, and the King will come back.'' He had the assurance that God would give the promised £100,000, which he would then invest in His work, and claim the hundredfold for fulfilling the Every Creature Commission.

Little did the company at the College realize that this was more than a victory meeting for finance: it was the completion of the earthly warfare of the Lord's intercessor. He, with the rest of the College, had faith for translation, and in the spirit of victory over death through Christ was awaiting the great day of His coming and the fulfillment of Philippians 3:21. But after gaining this final place of intercession, he accepted the will of God in fullness of victory. Within a month he was face to face with his Savior. Dr. Symonds, who was with him to the last, has given us this account:

"About two years prior to his home call, our beloved Director had a longing to pay a visit to the scenes of his meeting with the Holy Spirit in Llandrindod Wells. A few of us were privileged to accompany him. His soul was obviously blessed and revived as we stood outside the little chapel (now disused) where the Glorified Christ was revealed to him. Then he took us to the site of the convention tent, and told us once more of the way the Holy Ghost met him there in person and asked him for his body. As the Director thought again of those experiences, and of all that the Holy Ghost had done in and through him since, he was visibly strengthened in his believing that the Holy Ghost would never fail in the future to overcome all obstacles and reach every creature with the gospel in this generation.

"Shortly after that, I noticed as we climbed a hill an awful grayness came over him, and we had to halt for a while. He was in the throes of a heart attack. From that day onwards only a few of us knew how much he must have suffered. We tried to persuade him to take rest, but he was so consumed with his passion for the Kingdom and the dying souls of men that he never relaxed his grip on the prayer meetings and other business for his King, nor would he take any medicine to relieve his condition, preferring to leave all things, as always, to the Lord.

"From that Sunday night onwards, when there was such a victory of faith for finance, we were conscious that the Director felt his work on earth was finished. His main ministry had always been one of intercession. He often told me that he would now far rather go home to glory and leave the rest to such 'Joshuas' as God might call. His personal joy for all eternity would be that he had been faithful in the hands of God in laying the foundation. And thus it came to pass.

"On Tuesday, February 7, Miss Margaret Wright, the matron of the College hospital, had a special burden for him and went to his room after the evening meeting to see if he was all right. She found him pacing up and down the room, surprisingly singing some of the old Welsh hymns his mother used to sing of 'the land that is fairer than day.' One of them, translated into English, runs as follows:

> Fair and comely is my Savior,
> Fairest of the fair is He;
> King of kings I hail Him gladly
> Here and through eternity;
> His great beauty
> Has completely won my soul.
>
> See above the clouds and shadows,
> See, my soul, the Land of Light,
> Where the breeze is ever balmy,
> Where the sky is ever bright;
> Blessed myriads
> Now enjoy its perfect peace.
>
> Now at length a mighty rapture
> Thrills this troubled heart of mine,
> In the prospect of possessing
> This inheritance divine;
> Ever blessed
> They that seek this Land of Rest.

Yes, we part, but not for ever—
Joyful hopes our bosoms swell;
They who love the Savior never
Know a long, a last farewell!
Blissful unions
Lie beyond this parting veil.

"Next evening, February 8, at the close of the meeting, he seemed transported to glory. The whole company was standing and singing: 'Away over Jordan with my blessed Jesus'—the chorus he had chosen himself, but which had not been sung in the College for the past year. His face was described by some as reminding them of Stephen's—the face of an angel—as he took out his handkerchief and waved it while he sang. It seemed as if in greeting to his Savior and the saints gone on before. It was his last meeting on earth.

"Within half an hour I was called to see him as he lay prostrate on his bed in the throes of a terrible heart attack. To my amazement he consented to have some medication—the first foreboding to me that he did not really expect to recover. Had he expected recovery he would doubtless have preferred to hold on in naked faith.

"As he lay in an agony that I could only conjecture, for he never breathed one word to the very last with reference to his own suffering, he said, 'It is the Lord . . . it is the Lord . . . I am in the center of the Lord's will . . . everything is gained . . . it is the Lord.'

"During the following four days before he passed Home, whenever he came to consciousness it was to breathe out the name of some missionary (especially Mr. Norman Grubb and Mr. John Thomas), or other intimate friend for whom he was obviously praying, or to tell us of his believing of all the Vision.

"His last words came in a moment of consciousness on Sunday, February 12, as he recognized me and breathed in a quiet whisper, 'Victory . . . Hallelujah!' Several times during those days he had said that same word to Mrs. Howells—

'Glorious victory.' The end of his earthly pilgrimage came at 10 a.m. on Monday, February 13, 1950. As we knelt around his bed, we were deeply conscious of the marvelous presence of God. We breathed our prayer, 'Thy will be done,' and asked the Lord to make us worthy successors of such a noble servant of our Lord and Savior Jesus Christ."

Within an hour Mr. Samuel Howells had called the whole staff of the College and School together. Naturally quiet and retiring, it was obvious to all that the Spirit of God had come upon him as he summoned all to a rededication of their lives to carry through the vision and commission his father had laid down.

Following that day it was plain to everyone that in the hiddenness of the previous thirteen years, during which he had been with his father and mother in the College, God had been maturing and preparing His servant to take Mr. Howells' place. No son, by natural inheritance, could step into the place of such a father, but all recognized with thankfulness that the same divine Person who came to live in their late Director also indwelt his son, and thus College and School had the same Guide, Enabler and Supplier—the Lord Himself—in the midst.

This book was produced by the Christian Literature Crusade. We hope it has been helpful to you in living the Christian life. CLC is a literature mission with ministry in over 40 countries worldwide. If you would like to know more about us, or are interested in opportunities to serve with a faith mission, we invite you to write to:

Christian Literature Crusade
P.O. Box 1449
Fort Washington, PA 19034